LIBRARY

THE DALLAS PUBLIC LIBRARY:

CELEBRATING A CENTURY OF SERVICE, 1901–2001

The Dallas Public Library

CELEBRATING A CENTURY OF SERVICE
1901–2001

Michael V. Hazel

UNIVERSITY OF NORTH TEXAS PRESS • DENTON, TEXAS

Printed in the United States of America.

10 9 8 7 6 5 4 3 2 1

Permissions:
University of North Texas Press
P.O. Box 311336
Denton, TX 76203-1336

The paper used in this book meets the minimum requirements of the American National Standard for Permanence of Paper for Printed Library Materials, z39.48.1984. Binding materials have been chosen for durability.

Library of Congress Cataloging-in-Publication Data

Hazel, Michael V., 1948–
The Dallas Public Library : celebrating a century of service, 1901–2001 / Michael V. Hazel.
p. cm.
Includes bibliographical references (p.) and index.
ISBN 1-57441-141-1 (cloth : alk. paper)
1. Dallas Public Library—History. 2. Public libraries—Texas—Dallas—History—20th century. I. Title.

Z733.D14 H38 2001
027.4764'2812—dc21 2001027873

Design by Angela Schmitt

This book was made possible by generous grants from the Summerfield G. Roberts Foundation and the Friends of the Dallas Public Library, Inc.

Contents

LIST OF ILLUSTRATIONS

Preface

My introduction to the Dallas Public Library was the bookmobile that visited the Inwood Shopping Center once a week in the late 1950s. I was about eight or nine, and I have fond memories of standing in line, waiting my turn to climb the steps, and then browsing among the children's books on the shelves, attracted often by an intriguing title. When I was ten I was one of several students in my fifth-grade class who journeyed downtown to the Central Library to participate in Siddie Joe Johnson's creative writing classes. Miss Johnson encouraged my love of writing, which fairly quickly channeled itself into journalism and history rather than fiction, although my enjoyment of reading the latter remained keen. With my Dallas Public Library card, of course, I have enjoyed access to books of all classifications for more than forty years.

Since the new Central Library opened in 1982, I've utilized resources on all its floors, but my "home away from home" has been the Texas/Dallas History & Archives Division on the seventh floor. Nearly twenty years of researching, writing, and editing Dallas history wouldn't have been possible without its resources and the assistance of its staff. That proved especially true with this history of the library itself. The librarians in the division were unfailingly helpful in providing access to material documenting the institution's history, from brittle correspondence of 1900 through fascinating scrapbooks of the 1930s to published reports of more recent vintage.

I would also like to acknowledge my debt to Larry Grove's *Dallas Public Library: The First 75 Years.* Although I preferred to reference original sources whenever possible, Grove's entertaining book provided a helpful chronology and pointed me toward useful materials. I relied on his work more than my notes might indicate. Similarly, *Celebrating the First 50 Years: Friends of the Dallas Public Library,* by Lillian Moore Bradshaw, is a valuable resource in tracing the history of this important support group. Mrs. Bradshaw herself, of course, is perhaps the best living resource on the history of the Dallas Public Library. She generously answered questions for me, and I found the oral interview with her, conducted by Gerald Saxon in 1998, to be extremely helpful. I would also like to thank retired librarians Linda Allmand, Frances Bell, Tom Bogie, Byrdie Burras, Andrea Harris, David Henington, Fandella Meadows, Jan Moltzan, and Richard Waters for sharing their memories, and Library Director Ramiro Salazar and Assistant Director Joe Bearden for information and insights into the Dallas Public Library today and its plans for the future. I also want to acknowledge the careful copyediting provided by Richard Himmell, June Leftwich, and Carol Roark.

As librarian Cleora Clanton frequently pointed out in the 1930s, "Probably no institution in the city touches the lives of the citizens at more points than the public library." Certainly Dallas residents have recognized this fact, repeatedly approving by large majorities bond proposals to fund the construction of library facilities. For fifty years, thousands of patrons have supported the library through membership in the Friends of the Dallas Public Library. And, of course, for a century hundreds of thousands have utilized the library's resources for work, study, or pleasure. As one whose life has been immeasurably enriched by the Dallas Public Library, I am grateful to have had an opportunity to participate in celebrating its one hundredth anniversary by writing this history.

A note on illustrations: Unless otherwise credited, all illustrations appearing in this book come from the collections of the Dallas Public Library.

THE DALLAS PUBLIC LIBRARY:

CELEBRATING A CENTURY OF SERVICE, 1901–2001

Chapter 1

Building a Library

Civic leaders in Dallas viewed the coming of the twentieth century with optimism. Born as a frontier outpost on the banks of the Trinity River in 1841, Dallas had developed slowly as a market town and county seat until the railroads finally arrived in the 1870s. Overnight it became a boomtown, the transportation center for a rich agricultural region and a magnet for merchants and entrepreneurs. By 1890 Dallas was the largest city in Texas, with a population of more than 38,000. The "Panic of 1893" hit the city hard, bringing about a fall in the price of agricultural commodities, the failure of five local banks, and a drop in population. But within five years conditions were improving. Dallas was the leading book, drug, and jewelry market in the Southwest and had the largest retail trade of any city in the region. It was the world leader in the manufacture and sale of saddlery and the leading market for cotton gin machinery. Local boosters liked to compare Dallas to prominent Midwestern cities like St. Louis and Cincinnati, and called it "The Queen City of the Southwest."

But civic leaders in Dallas recognized that their city needed intellectual as well as economic resources if it was to compete on a national scale. And it lacked one resource that was coming to be accepted as essential: a free public library. How a public

In 1899 Dallas was a bustling metropolis, with streetcars criss-crossing its substantial business district.

library was built in Dallas is the story of a group of dedicated individuals who mobilized public opinion, won the support of a wealthy philanthropist, and constructed a model facility in an amazingly short period of time.

There had been "public libraries" in Dallas since the 1870s, but like most libraries in the United States, they were really private libraries, open only to those who paid a subscription. One of these, founded by Colonel John C. McCoy in 1884, began above a music store on Main Street and later moved to the city hall with more than 1,600 books.[1] Another, under the auspices of the Pierian Club, a women's literary society, was housed in the home of Mrs. Richard W. Allen on Fairmount Street; the club later donated their volumes as the nucleus for a traveling library in rural areas.[2] The development of the public school district after 1884 increased the demand for library facilities, especially since the only reference books in the high school library when it opened were an encyclopedia and dictionary furnished by the principal and superintendent.[3]

As Dallas continued to grow, attracting residents from the North and East, the lack of a public library began to appear as a hindrance to the city's efforts to promote itself as a center for culture and civilized life. "Pauline Periwinkle" (Mrs. S. Isadore Miner), a columnist for *The Dallas Morning News* who promoted a long list of civic improvement projects, reminded her readers in 1897 that "the stranger in a small town is often surprised by the size and completeness of a library that gives him an opinion of the progress of its people no other enterprise could have provoked."[4] The Commercial Club, a forerunner of the chamber of commerce, concurred, adopting a resolution in 1898 endorsing the movement for a library. "There is no other city of the size of Dallas in the United States," proclaimed the club's president, Charles L. Wakefield, "which does not have at least one good public library."[5]

One problem was that until the late nineteenth century, municipalities usually viewed their responsibilities as limited to maintaining public safety and providing basic services such as a water supply. Supporting cultural institutions like libraries was an alien concept. This was beginning to change, however, as people began to view a library as the visible proof of their community's commitment to literacy and education. The new city charter for Dallas, adopted in 1898, authorized the expenditure of $2,000 in tax revenues to maintain a library, but Dallas still faced the issue of providing a permanent home for a public library.

Andrew Carnegie's decision to donate a large part of his fortune to building public libraries provided an obvious opportunity. Feeling an obligation to share his wealth, and grateful for his own self-education through books, the steel magnate built eight libraries in the United States (six of them in Pennsylvania) between 1886 and 1897. In 1898 he supported three more, one of them in Atlanta and another in the small East Texas town of Pittsburg. Word started to spread that funds were available, and towns throughout the nation began formulating requests.[6]

Civic leaders in Dallas had always prided themselves on reacting quickly to take advantage of opportunities to enhance their city. In the early

Among the early attempts at a public library in Dallas was one in the 1880s by attorney John McCoy in this block on Main Street near Field (next to Frees & Son in this photo). It survived only a few years.

1870s they had enticed two railroads to pass through Dallas, making it the first rail crossroads in Texas and insuring its position as the transportation and trading center for North Texas. In the 1880s they had organized the State Fair of Texas, bringing thousands of visitors to Dallas each October and greatly benefiting local businesses. In 1889 they had even annexed the neighboring town of East Dallas so that Dallas would rank as the largest city in Texas on the 1890 Federal Census. Now they moved swiftly to secure Carnegie support for a public library building.

Writing under the penname of "Pauline Periwinkle" for The Dallas Morning News, *Mrs. S. Isadore Miner championed a wide range of progressive reforms for the city, including the construction of a public library. She also served for many years as a library trustee. (Photo courtesy of the Dallas Historical Society)*

Dallas clubwomen actually initiated the movement, led by May Dickson Exall. Mrs. Exall was born in McKinney, Texas, in 1859. Her father, an army captain, was killed at the Battle of Shiloh. In 1875 her mother left McKinney, taking her two children East, where her son entered the Naval Academy and May enrolled at Vassar. The family returned to Texas and settled in Dallas in 1883. May Dickson was probably among the minority of college-educated women in Dallas at the time, and when the Dallas Shakespeare Club was formed in 1886, its members elected her their president, paying tribute to her intellectual superiority as well as to her leadership position. Mrs. Exall (as she became after marrying Henry Exall in 1887) reigned as president of the Shakespeare Club for the next fifty years.[7]

In November 1898, Mrs. Exall invited representatives of several other clubs to meet and organize a Dallas Federation of Women's Clubs. Similar federations were being organized around the country as clubwomen began to focus their attention on community problems. Acting at first individually, the women soon discovered that their effectiveness was increased as they banded together. The first project adopted by the Dallas Federation was

Andrew Carnegie's grants funded the construction of public libraries throughout the United States. Dallas was among his early beneficiaries.

the securing of a public library for Dallas.[8]

The Federation officially adopted this goal at a meeting March 1, 1899, at the Oriental Hotel, Dallas's most ornate hostelry. Four days later, the Federation published a letter in *The Dallas Morning News* announcing that the women's clubs "have determined to help the citizens of Dallas help themselves in providing a public library, which is one of the necessities of this thriving city. . . ." Wasting no time, delegates of the Federation met the next day with representatives of the school board in order to obtain their support. Out of this meeting came two committees, one to locate a suitable site for a library building, and the other a ways and means committee to study the financial aspects.[9] On March 12 the *Dallas News*, the city's leading newspaper, came out strongly in favor of the project. "The absence of a public library in Dallas has been remarked with humiliation by the citizen and astonishment by strangers and visitors," the editors noted. "The public institutions of a city are an index to the character of its citizenship, and a thoroughly appointed and well patronized public library is considered significant of the culture and intellectual standing of its people."[10]

The State Fair of Texas drew thousands of visitors to Dallas each October beginning in 1886.

The Dallas Public Library Association was formally launched at a public meeting March 30 at the Commercial Club. J. M. Howell, president of the Dallas School Board, chaired the meeting, with Mrs. Miner ("Pauline Periwinkle") acting as secretary. The meeting adopted a constitution and elected nine directors: Mrs. Exall; Mrs. J. R. Currie, president of Pierian Club; Mrs. Sidney Smith, president of the Standard Club; Mrs. Jules Schneider, president of the Ladies Musicale; Mrs. George K.

May Dickson Exall organized Dallas clubwomen to campaign for a public library, and she served as the first president of the Dallas Public Library Association. (Photo courtesy of Betty May Exall Stewart)

Meyer, vice president of Pierian; Mr. Howell of the School Board; and businessmen E. M. Kahn, L. M. Dabney, and C. L. Wakefield.[11] At a subsequent meeting, Mrs. Exall was elected president and Mrs. Currie, vice president.

Three trustees were also selected to hold title to funds and property until the library was constructed and turned over to the city. These were Joseph M. Dickson, an attorney and Mrs. Exall's brother; Jules Schneider, a wealthy businessman; and Alexander Sanger, co-owner of Sanger Brothers Store, the city's leading retail establishment. Discussions with the city council soon obtained a pledge of a lot on Commerce Street near Akard, on which the directors of the Library Association contemplated constructing a building for $10,000. The city also agreed to provide $2,000 annually toward the library's maintenance.[12]

Built in 1893 at the corner of Commerce and Akard streets, the Oriental Hotel was Dallas's finest hostelry for twenty years and the site of the meeting at which the Dallas Federation of Women's Clubs officially adopted the goal of achieving a public library for the city.

Although the directors planned to apply to Carnegie for assistance, they understood that he favored projects in cities that had demonstrated their commitment to building and maintaining a library by first raising funds locally. Thus the organized campaign launched by the Dallas Library Association. The first contribution was fifty cents from Adamo Janelli, an Italian immigrant who had founded the Dallas chapter of the Salvation Army on a street corner in 1899. Major impetus for the drive was provided by Colonel Alfred H. Belo, publisher of *The Dallas Morning News*, who pledged $1,000.[13] His donation was matched by businessmen John S. Armstrong, Colonel W. E. Hughes, the Sanger Brothers, and Colonel C. C. Slaughter, each of whom also contributed $1,000. Dallas schoolteachers donated $500. At a large women's meeting on May 10 at the First Christian Church, Mrs. Exall was able to report that nearly $6,000 had been raised. At this meeting, the city was divided

Alexander Sanger, co-owner of Dallas's leading department store, served on the three-man finance committee for the construction of the new library and then on the library's board of trustees. The library's South Dallas branch was later named for him.

into districts, and women were assigned to canvas assigned areas for donations.[14]

Meanwhile, Pauline Periwinkle had written letters to more than a hundred prominent citizens soliciting their support. Many of their responses were published in *The Dallas Morning News* during April, keeping the project before the public and creating the impression of a groundswell of support. Former Governor Barnett Gibbs, for instance, pledged twenty-five volumes from his own collection to the new library and offered to pay monthly dues for its upkeep.[15] George T. Winston, president of the University of Texas, offered a simple but eloquent plea: "The free school, the free library, and the free press are the three great institutions of popular education and popular power. Dallas now has two of these—the third should be provided!"[16]

With close to $12,000 raised by mid-summer, the directors of the Library Association decided it was time to approach Andrew Carnegie. Extra motivation was no doubt provided by the announcement on June 30 that Carnegie had just granted Fort Worth $50,000. The neighboring cities had been rivals practically since their founding half a century earlier. As Mrs. Exall recalled, "Dallas, usually a leader, must not be outdone."[17] In fact, in the opening paragraph of the letter she wrote to Carnegie on behalf of the Library Association, Mrs. Exall referred to "your munificent gift to our neighboring city of Ft. Worth, a town of about half the size of Dallas." She went on to review the history of the movement for a Dallas library, and the funds raised so far. She described the economic development of the city during the past quarter century and its upstanding residents, assuring Carnegie, "Our citizenry are characterized by industry and sobriety and there is nothing in Dallas of the wild frontier town."[18]

"I well remember how I labored over the wording of this letter," she later recalled, "not stopping to think it would never come under the eye of the Honorable Andrew, but would be coldly perused by his Secretary, who would, doubtless, be empowered to give the decision, so momentous to our organization."[19] She sent the letter off on August 7, then she had an anxious wait until early September, when Carnegie's answer was forwarded to her while she was on vacation. "Surely I shall do for Dallas what I did for Fort Worth," Carnegie wrote, indicating an awareness of the local rivalry, "especially since your library association has succeeded in raising $11,000." He agreed to provide up to $50,000 for construction of a library, if the city would donate a lot and increase its commitment from $2,000 to $4,000 per year, which he felt was more realistic for a city the size of Dallas.[20]

Mrs. Exall kept the good news a secret until she returned to Dallas and then announced it at a meeting of the Library Association on September 19. The city's reaction, understandably, was ecstatic, and Carnegie's name rang with praises. "Every public spirited man, woman, and child in the city," reported the *Dallas Times Herald*, "felt a thrill of enthusiasm at the latest manifestation of the great iron man's unselfish love of the public weal."[21] At a meeting two days later in the city hall auditorium, with every seat filled and people standing in the rear, Carnegie's gift was officially accepted on behalf of the city by Mayor John H. Traylor, motions of appreciation were passed, and the name of the Dallas Library Association was changed to the Carnegie Public Library Association.

Because the current Dallas city charter limited the annual support for a library to $2,000, the city council submitted a resolution to the State Legislature asking for an amendment rais-

Colonel Alfred H. Belo, publisher of The Dallas Morning News, *launched the drive for the Dallas Public Library with a $1,000 donation. He later contributed funds to start the book collection. (Photo courtesy of the Belo Archives)*

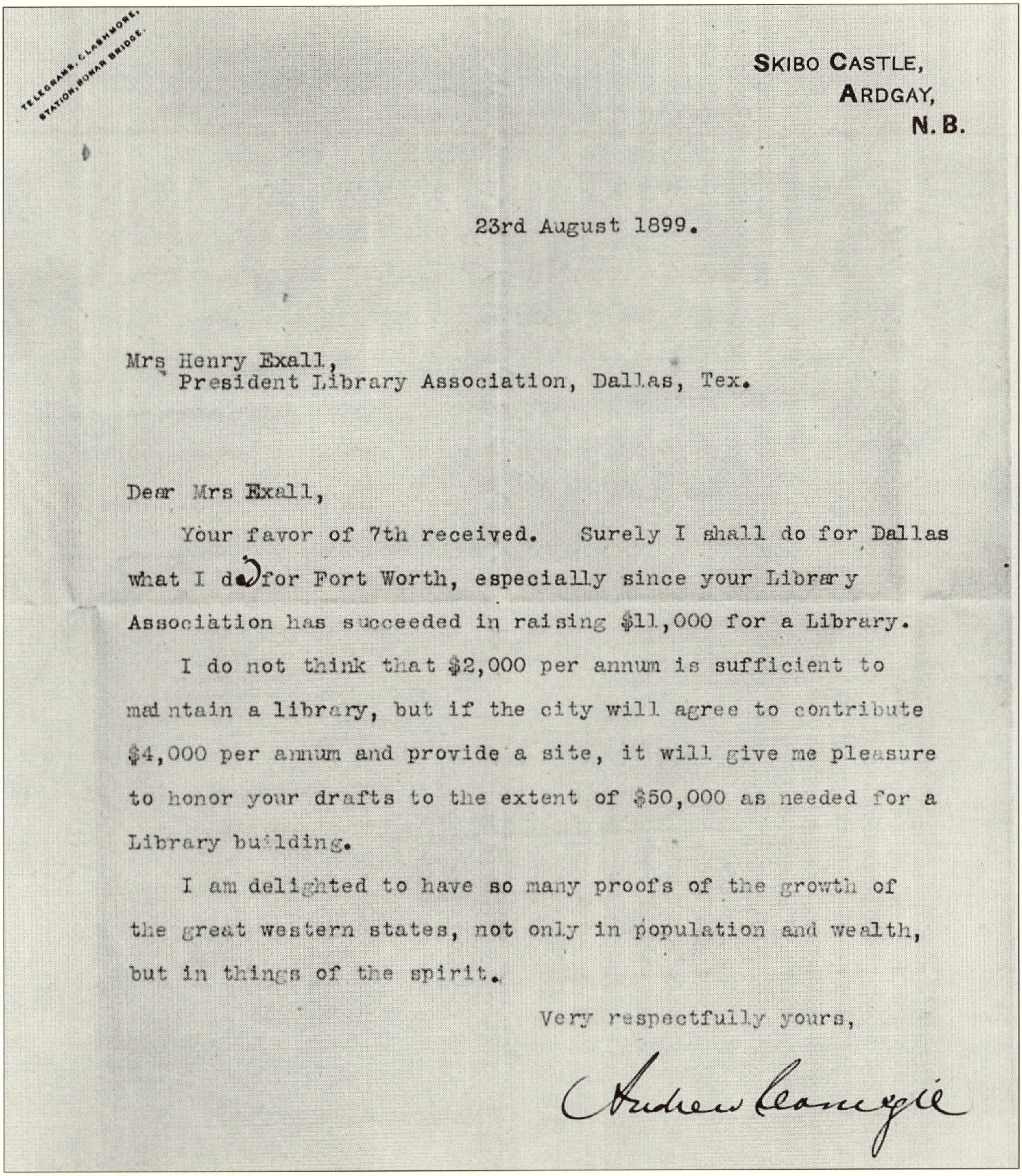

TELEGRAMS, CLASHMORE,
STATION, BONAR BRIDGE.

SKIBO CASTLE,
ARDGAY,
N. B.

23rd August 1899.

Mrs Henry Exall,
President Library Association, Dallas, Tex.

Dear Mrs Exall,

Your favor of 7th received. Surely I shall do for Dallas what I do for Fort Worth, especially since your Library Association has succeeded in raising $11,000 for a Library.

I do not think that $2,000 per annum is sufficient to maintain a library, but if the city will agree to contribute $4,000 per annum and provide a site, it will give me pleasure to honor your drafts to the extent of $50,000 as needed for a Library building.

I am delighted to have so many proofs of the growth of the great western states, not only in population and wealth, but in things of the spirit.

Very respectfully yours,

Andrew Carnegie

Andrew Carnegie's letter to Mrs. Exall, announcing his pledge of $50,000 to build a library in Dallas, was published in the local newspapers on September 19, 1899.

ing that figure to $4,000. Henry Exall enlisted the support of Governor Joseph D. Sayers, and C. L. Wakefield made a special trip to Austin to lobby the legislators. The charter amendment was approved early in the 1900 legislative session.[22]

Carnegie's gift meant that the Library Association could plan for a much larger structure than the one it had originally envisioned. The lot on Commerce Street that had been offered by the city was now deemed to be too small, so it was sold and the proceeds invested in a larger property at the corner of Commerce and Harwood. Total cost of the land, measuring 100 feet wide by 200 feet deep, was $9,525, with the Library Association contributing about $6,000.[23]

A public competition was then held to select the architectural plans. Of the thirteen sets submitted, the review committee selected those of Marshall R. Sanguinet of Fort Worth. The identities of the architects had been kept secret until after the committee made its choice. "Imagine our surprise and consternation," recalled Mrs. Exall, "when it was discovered that plan No. 6, so decidedly the favorite, was submitted by a firm of Ft. Worth architects." Because of the rivalry between Dallas and Fort Worth, she explained, "it seemed a tragedy that five plans submitted by Dallas architects should be turned down" in favor of a Fort Worth one. So the committee went over the plans again, only to discover that their second choice was also by Sanguinet and his partner, Carl Staats. At that point, they were forced to set aside local prejudice and accept what was clearly the superior plan.[24]

Fort Worth architect Marshall Sanguinet won the contest to design the new library for Dallas.

John Lawrence Mauran, a St. Louis architect who served on the selection committee, described Sanguinet's plans as "dignified, pleasing to the eye, well ventilated and structurally

Rosa Leeper became the first librarian of the Dallas Public Library in October 1900 and directed the institution until 1916.

well conceived."[25] Adhering to formal, neoclassical designs, the front of the building was dominated by pairs of Ionic columns, two stories high, supporting an entablature. Arches over the entry door and ground-floor windows softened the otherwise severe façade. The building would front on Commerce Street (about ninety-three feet wide) and stretch 114 feet back on Harwood. The main construction contract was let to Sonnefield & Emmins of Dallas for $43,232.10 on October 10, 1900, and the cornerstone was laid on January 16, 1901, with Episcopal Bishop Alexander Garrett delivering a forceful and inspired invocation.[26]

Even before construction began, the Library Association had hired a librarian, Miss Rosa Leeper. A native Texan, Miss Leeper had six years' experience as an assistant librarian in St. Louis. She visited twenty public libraries throughout the United States, studying their procedures, before she assumed her duties in Dallas in October 1900. Mrs. Exall described her as possessing "executive ability, a wide acquaintance with books, an ardent interest in her work, and, above all, a keen realization of the high mission of a librarian." [27]

To assist Miss Leeper in selecting books for the library, the library board appointed a committee including three of its members—Mrs. Exall, Mrs. Smith, and Alexander Sanger—and several other knowledgeable citizens. Their first order was for 1,300 books, costing about $7,000, paid for from the funds remaining after paying for the building site. Colonel Belo contributed $500 to buy books, and other individuals donated money and books, so that by the time the library opened, there were 9,852 volumes on the shelves.[28]

The library board also compiled the first "Rules and Regulations" for use of the library. The library would be open seven days a week, although no books could be issued on Sunday "for home use." No person "who is intoxicated or unclean in person or dress" would be admitted to the library, nor would smoking or eating be allowed. "Loud conversation" was forbidden. Those living within three and a half miles of the Dallas post office could borrow books, and there were even provisions for "temporary sojourners" to obtain privileges. All uses of the library, however, were restricted to "white persons of good deportment, character and habits."[29]

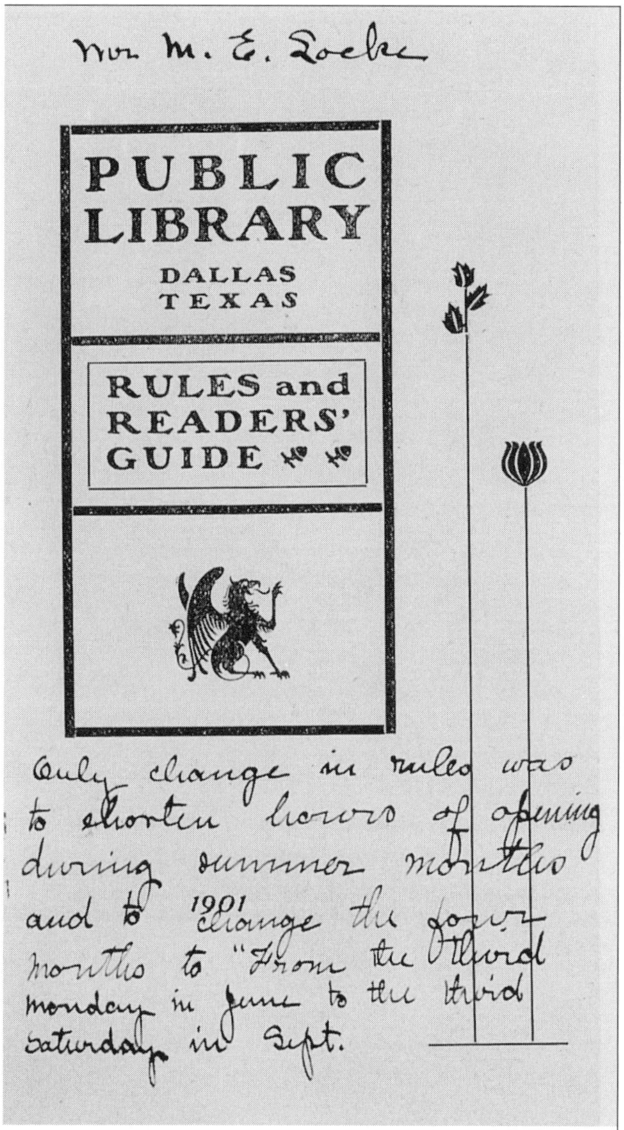

The library's board of trustees published the first "Rules and Readers' Guide" in 1901.

Meanwhile construction continued apace. The building committee, chaired by Joseph Dickson, watched expenses so carefully that the total cost came to \$50,097, only \$97 over the amount donated by Andrew Carnegie.[30] This had to be one of the lowest cost overruns on a municipal project in the city's history.

On October 28, 1901, the Library Association extended a cordial invitation "to all the citizens of Dallas and vicinity, including Oak Cliff" (referring to the independent municipality west of the Trinity River), to attend the formal opening of the library at 8:30 P.M. Tuesday, October 29. The guests walked up the steps, between the columns of Bedford stone, into a rotunda with marble floor and wainscoting. A newspaper reporter gushed that it was "probably the most beautiful library building in the South."[31] A general reading room lay on one side of the hall, with a special children's room opposite. The checkout desk was directly ahead. Upstairs was an Art Room, where a public exhibition was scheduled to open a few days later. Also on the second floor was an assembly hall, known as "Carnegie Hall," where a brief opening ceremony took place, featuring remarks by Mrs. Exall and other

Library Association representatives, and official acceptance of the library by Mayor Ben Cabell.

In her remarks at the opening, Mrs. Exall described the children's room as "perhaps the most attractive spot in our building," adorned with reproductions of famous artwork. "There is to me no more inspiring thought in connection with our work than this, that no child in Dallas need any longer be deprived of the privilege of reading good and attractive books." The Library Association, in fact, saw the entire facility as a democratic institution. "In past centuries a library was a store house for the conservation of books, rather than for the diffusion of knowledge," Mrs. Exall remarked. "It is the aim and object of the modern library to have its books circulated as widely as possible so as to act as a leaven on the whole community."[32]

In less than two and a half years, the Library Association, founded and largely driven by Dallas clubwomen, had succeeded in organizing and building a public library, a task that had defeated all previous attempts. Some of the credit was due, of course, to Andrew Carnegie, whose generous gift made possible the construction of a facility that was to serve the city for the next fifty years. The Library Association honored his role by inscribing over the entrance the words, "Donated to the City of Dallas by Andrew Carnegie." But the lion's share of the credit belongs to the dedicated women, led by Mrs. Exall, who perceived a need in their community and worked tirelessly until it was met.

Looking from the circulation desk toward the front door, the double staircase leading to the second level is visible.

The challenge now would be to nurture the library and keep it growing.

•

The main reading room was located to the left of the lobby as patrons entered the library.

The check-out desk greeted visitors as they entered the library.

(right) The auditorium on the second floor of the library was named Carnegie Hall in honor of the building's patron.

(below) The children's room was originally located to the right of the lobby.

During its early years, the library still had private residences as its neighbors on Commerce Street, as this photograph indicates. By the 1910s, commercial development dominated the area.

Chapter 2

Growing Pains

The new library enjoyed enormous popularity from the beginning. During the first ten weeks, nearly 3,000 people obtained library cards, and more than 15,000 books were checked out. The children's collection attracted especially heavy use, as school principals sent classes to the library, and teachers presented lectures on art and music in the children's room. Mrs. Mary K. Craig, a prominent Dallas educator, inaugurated a series of talks to children in February 1902; the next month, 500 children showed up, forcing the program upstairs to Carnegie Hall.[1]

The library eschewed old-fashioned printed catalogs and adopted the modern Dewey Decimal system for its books. "The catalog so far has not progressed beyond the author and title stage," Miss Leeper wrote in a report to *The Library Journal*, "though some subjects of local interest, such as cotton, Mexico, the race question, Texas history, and all biography have been brought out."[2]

With the library open, several patrons donated valuable collections of books. Especially significant were 167 volumes of French literature contributed by Julian Reverchon, a noted botanist. His father had brought the books from France in the 1850s and carried them in a spring wagon from the Texas coast to the utopian La Reunion settlement near Dallas. E. H. R. ("Ned")

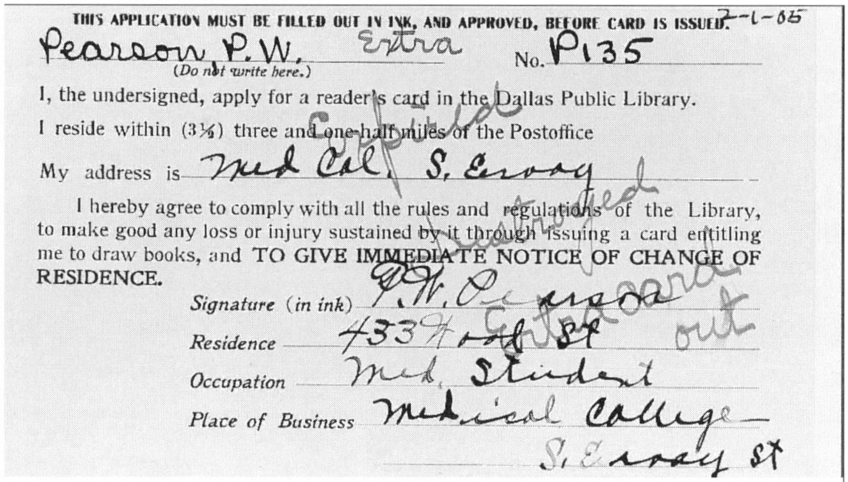
THIS APPLICATION MUST BE FILLED OUT IN INK, AND APPROVED, BEFORE CARD IS ISSUED. 2-1-05

Pearson, P.W. Extra No. P135

(Do not write here.)

I, the undersigned, apply for a reader's card in the Dallas Public Library.

I reside within (3½) three and one-half miles of the Postoffice

My address is Med Col, S. Ervay

I hereby agree to comply with all the rules and regulations of the Library, to make good any loss or injury sustained by it through issuing a card entitling me to draw books, and TO GIVE IMMEDIATE NOTICE OF CHANGE OF RESIDENCE.

Signature (in ink) P.W. Pearson

Residence 433½ [illegible] St

Occupation Med. Student

Place of Business Medical College — S. Ervay St

Early patrons of the Dallas Public Library had to fill out an application form in order to obtain a "reader's card." A medical student submitted this one in 1905.

Green, the man who drove the first gasoline-powered automobile into Dallas in 1899, also donated books from his collection.[3] Financial gifts to the book fund included $1,000 from the family of Colonel A. H. Belo, who died in April 1901, and $1,000 from Miss Helen Gould. Philip Sanger, one of the Sanger brothers who owned Dallas's leading emporium, left $1,000 to the library upon his death in 1902.[4]

Like most librarians, Rosa Leeper appears to have viewed her role as a combination of educator and missionary. Many patrons asked only for the latest works by popular novelists. Miss Leeper was determined to raise their sights. "To the mentally halt, lame and blind still asking for books by Mary Cecil Hay, Bertha M. Clay, and Mrs. Southworth," she explained, "we give books selected from our class 'First Aid to the Injured.'" Through her efforts, she was pleased to report, William Dean Howells "has been discovered several times, and great has been the joy of the discoverer."[5]

Just teaching patrons how to use the library's resources took time. "Four out of five persons using the library for reference work," Miss Leeper wrote, "either hesitate to let it be known what they want or are unable to express that want." Once the librarian figured out what the user needed, she still had to open the book and point to the relevant passage. "The young people we try to teach something of the use of books," she explained. "For the older ones, it is generally more economy of time and patience to do the work."[6]

By May 1903 the library was on its third registration book. The first one had allowed space for the names of only 5,000 borrowers; the second had room for 8,000. Now the librarians were

As patrons obtained cards to use the Dallas Public Library, their names were entered in a registration book. Mrs. Henry Exall and her son, Henry, Jr., were the first people with the initial "E" to register.

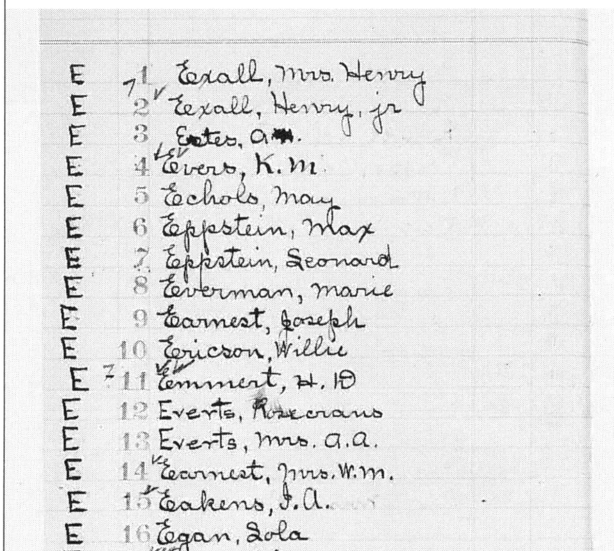
E 1 Exall, Mrs. Henry
E 2 Exall, Henry, jr
E 3 Estes, A. [illegible]
E 4 Evers, K. M.
E 5 Echols, May
E 6 Eppstein, Max
E 7 Eppstein, Leonard
E 8 Everman, Marie
E 9 Earnest, Joseph
E 10 Ericson, Willie
E 11 Emmert, H. B
E 12 Everts, Rosecrans
E 13 Everts, Mrs. A. A.
E 14 Earnest, Mrs. W. M.
E 15 Eakens, J. A.
E 16 Egan, Lola
E 17 Evers, Volney
E 18 Excalotta, Francis
E 19 Evans, Louise
E 20 Eastman, Mrs. Ralph
E 21 Evans, C. J.
E 22 Everett, Louise
E 23 Elderkin, Jean R.
E 24 Estes, Annie
E 25 Englich, S. P.
E 26 Edwards, Mrs A. B.
E 27 Elliott, R. S.
E 28 Emery, J. W.
E 29 Evans, Miss Annie
E 30 Evans, C. Gwynne
E 31 Edwards, G. C.
E 32 Evans, Charles
E 33 ~~Estes, Frank~~ Estes, F
E 34 Elwood, Miss Edith
E 35 Ellison, Floyd

planning for 15,000.[7] After the first hectic months, Miss Leeper was able to report that work in the children's department had "now about reached normal." "The behavior is good, and though we can't brag about the non-fiction issue, the care taken in selecting books for this department is a guarantee that the books read are wholesome and clean." The main problem was that "little people are hard on books," and the library needed funds for replacing worn volumes. As for the rest of the library, the greatest need was for sets of magazines. "It is positively maddening," Miss Leeper wrote, "to find long lists of references in Poole to articles in the *Nation*, *North American Review*, *Popular Science Monthly*, and other magazines of that class and then to have to explain we haven't got them."[8]

Miss Leeper handled the work load with only two regular assistants, one extra assistant, a young man who worked evenings and Sundays, and a janitor. For budgetary reasons, the library hired untrained assistants, who were paid twenty dollars a month. "One disadvantage of this plan," Miss Leeper complained, "is that it sometimes takes months to prove that an assistant cannot get beyond the simplest routine work, and another is that just when a promising assistant is beginning to be of real use she sometimes marries."[9] Both of these situations had occurred, resulting in frequent replacement of assistants.

Demands on the library increased as Dallas experienced rapid growth during the first decade of the new century. The population, which stood at 42,638 in 1900, would more than double by 1910. Located at the center of a transportation network of railroads and, increasingly, highways, Dallas was the central distribution point for all North Texas for manufactured goods. It was also becoming the center for banking and insurance in the Southwest and was the leading inland cotton market in the world. Miss Leeper was proud of the reference support the library provided to businesses, not only in Dallas but also in the surrounding region. "We want it known that the men of the community, of whatever business or profession, have a right to the services of the institution which they are supporting, and that the Library is ready to serve them," she wrote. Members of literary clubs, debate students, and a host of others were also frequent users of the library.[10]

The $4,000 provided annually by the city for library support had quickly become inadequate. What the public didn't always understand was that the library budget not only had to pay staff, purchase new books, and maintain subscriptions to periodicals, but also repair or replace worn books. "Each year we must see a larger proportion of our book fund used for replacements," Miss Leeper explained, "a proof not only of the use of books, but of the judiciousness of the original selection, as we do not replace books of merely ephemeral value." Users also wanted the library open longer hours, but this would mean additional staff.[11]

Philip Sanger and his brother Alexander followed the railroad to Dallas in 1872 and opened the town's largest emporium, Sanger Brothers. Both brothers were strong supporters of civic improvements, including the public library.

In 1907 Dallas voters approved a new city charter that instituted a commission form of government. The library trustees took advantage of this opportunity to secure a change in their funding; instead of a fixed amount annually, the library would receive one and a half cents per hundred dollars in tax valuation. In its first year of operation, this alteration produced $7,438.82 for the library budget.[12]

The increased operating funds, however, did nothing to alleviate space problems. The library's collections doubled during the first five years, straining the available shelf space. The reference

By 1910 Dallas was a thriving metropolis, complete with a fourteen-story "skyscraper," the Praetorian Building, from which this photograph was taken, looking west down Main Street. The arch in the foreground was erected for an Elks convention in 1908 and proved so popular it stayed up for two years.

room was overcrowded with both researchers and materials. The children's room was too small to accommodate all the requested uses. The local medical association asked to establish its headquarters upstairs and place its valuable medical library there. The library, only six years old, was already running out of room. The library trustees felt it was premature to consider constructing branch libraries, so they drew up plans for an addition to the back of the building, on vacant land that had been acquired with the possibility of an extension in mind.

Mrs. Exall wrote to Andrew Carnegie in May 1907, requesting $35,000 for this extension. Carnegie declined the appeal. According to his secretary, James Bertram, Carnegie felt the original building was still large enough for strictly library uses. "He is not building medical libraries, nor art rooms, club rooms, etc.," Bertram explained. If the library needed more space, then it should expand into the art department and classrooms. Lectures could be given in the basement, and the present assembly room ("Carnegie Hall") could also be used for library purposes. If none of these measures sufficed, then the board should consider erecting a branch library elsewhere in the city.[13]

The Public Art Gallery was the first to go. This space had been suggested by a popular local artist, Frank Reaugh, when the library was being planned. At the time, Dallas had no permanent gallery where residents could view fine art. Since the library planners wanted to construct a building large enough to accommodate future growth, but didn't have immediate need for much of the space on the second floor, Reaugh felt some of this area might

During the early twentieth century, Dallas was the transportation center for North Texas, served by nine railroads. The Missouri-Kansas-Texas terminal, pictured here, was one of five passenger depots downtown.

be well devoted to a gallery. The library trustees accepted Reaugh's suggestion and appointed an art committee, chaired by Mrs. Exall and including prominent clubwomen Mrs. W. H. Abrams, Mrs. Jules Schneider, and Mrs. Sydney Smith; Mrs. Smith for some years had helped organize art exhibits at the annual State Fair in Dallas. The art committee organized an exhibition to coincide with the grand opening of the library in 1901. The gallery itself was located on the second floor, at the top of the stairs. It was a large room, with red walls, chairs arranged down the center, and electric light bulbs supplementing natural light from the skylights.

The inaugural art exhibit included mostly works that had recently been displayed at the State Fair, but it also included new entries by such prominent Texas artists as painter Robert Onderdonk and sculptor Elisabet Ney. Frank Reaugh himself contributed five paintings. The art committee decided to charge admission to the exhibit, twenty-five cents for adults and ten cents for children. "The money obtained by this exhibit goes to form the nucleus of an art fund for . . . purchases," explained the newspapers. "A citizen of Dallas has offered to give half of any amount raised for purchases."[14] The unidentified citizen was John S. Armstrong, a merchant and owner of a meat-packing firm, who was soon to begin development of the Highland Park residential suburb. More than 1,000 people viewed the exhibit before it closed, but after paying expenses, the art fund was left with only $175. However, Mrs. Exall mentioned the art fund to Mrs. A. H. Belo, "who in her quiet, modest way, was ever ready to give gen-

Before World War I, Dallas was the largest inland cotton market in the world. Brokers, including many from Europe, conducted business at the Dallas Cotton Exchange, above.

erous aid to any good cause." "Imagine my surprise," recalled Mrs. Exall, "when the next day a check came from Mrs. Belo to start an art fund."[15] This enabled the committee to call on Mr. Armstrong for his matching pledge (limited to $500). The committee then began formulating an acquisitions policy to build a permanent collection.

After another successful exhibit in 1902, from which the art committee purchased several paintings, the time seemed ripe to form an independent organization that could direct the creation of a permanent art gallery. In January 1903, twenty-five citizens formed the Dallas Art Association, with Mrs. Charles L. Dexter as president. During the next few years, the Dallas Art Association mounted several exhibitions at the library, presented public lectures and musical programs, and acquired more paintings. But by 1908 enthusiasm seemed to be waning. Membership had actually dropped. Some of the directors felt the problem lay in the gallery itself. The space was limited, as were the viewing hours. The Fair Park Association had just built a brick, fireproof Fine Arts Building at Fair Park. Mrs. George K. Meyer presented the trustees with a plan to transfer title of the art collection to the City of Dallas in return for use of the new building as an art museum. Under the agreement, the Art Association would remain trustee for the collection and sole selector of what works would be added to it.[16] Since the library now needed the gallery space for its own uses, this seemed a good solution for both groups.

The paintings were transferred to the new Dallas Public Art Gallery at Fair Park, which opened with much fanfare on April

The library staff prided itself on serving the needs of a diverse public. Businessmen, such as those pictured in the main reading room, kept up with the latest financial and economic news through the library's periodicals.

Without an adequate library in the public high school, students flocked to the Carnegie Library to study and do research. These girls are pictured in the reference room.

Local artist Frank Reaugh proposed designating space on the second floor of the Carnegie Library for an art gallery, and he donated a painting to start the collection. (Photo courtesy of Bob Reitz)

17, 1909. It was the first public art gallery south of St. Louis except for the one at New Orleans. It subsequently underwent several name changes, first to the Dallas Museum of Fine Arts and, most recently, to the Dallas Museum of Art. It also moved several times before settling into its latest home in 1984, back downtown, only a few blocks from where it started in 1901.[17]

The principal dissenter to the move was Frank Reaugh, who felt that Fair Park was too far away and the museum should remain downtown. Since he had donated a painting, *On the Road to the Brazos* to the library in 1902, before the Art Association was formed, he insisted that it remain in the library. It is still there, on the seventh floor of the J. Erik Jonsson Central Library building.

The children's library was moved into the vacated art room. A few years later, the lecture hall on the second floor was also given up, and the reference department was moved there. This latter move solved a critical problem. Miss Leeper had reported in 1908 that the stacks in the reference area were so crowded, there was no room to shelve current bound periodicals. "Our public documents fill five large stacks and are piled three deep on the tops of eleven others in the stack room."[18] These shifts brought the library some breathing room, at least for a few years. Since it now seemed apparent that the library would not be expanding to the rear, Dallas clubwomen landscaped the lot behind the building with shrubs and a bed of roses. "In the hot days of summer," remarked Mrs. Exall, "amid the rush and roar of the city, it presents a pleasing and restful sight to the eye."[19] Another refresher came in 1916: "In accordance with the city ordinance abolishing

The Dallas Museum of Art had its beginnings in the "Public Art Gallery" located on the second floor of the Carnegie Library. In 1910 the gallery moved to the new Fine Arts Building at Fair Park.

the public drinking cup," reported the librarian, "a bubbling fountain has been installed in each library building."[20]

After serving as president of the Dallas Library Association's board of trustees for more than ten years, Mrs. Exall submitted her resignation in January 1910. Her only brother, Joseph Dickson, who had been of such help during the campaign to construct the library, had recently died. This event, she explained, "brought such great sorrow into my life" that she no longer felt up to heading the library.[21] Her fellow trustees at first declined to accept her resignation and asked her to reconsider, but she was adamant.[22] She did, however, remain a trustee for several more years. Attorney Maurice E. Locke, the vice president, succeeded Mrs. Exall as president and served until his death in 1919. He, in turn, was succeeded by his vice president, Edward A. Belsterling.

Another significant change in the leadership of the library came in June 1916, when Rosa Leeper requested a leave of absence for one year. Miss Leeper had directed the library for fifteen years, helping to plan it, hiring and supervising its staff, managing it with frugal budgets, coping with space limitations. The years had taken their toll. Miss Leeper needed a rest, "for the Library's good, and my own," as she put it. The board approved her request and appointed Miss Betsy Wiley as acting librarian.[23] Miss Leeper set out on a trip to California and the Orient. After a few months, she decided not to return to Dallas and submitted her resignation. The board held on to her resignation for several months but finally, in May 1917, the trustees accepted it. They passed a resolution saluting her loyalty, industry, and efficiency, which had "contributed to a five-fold increase of

The busy children's department moved upstairs into the old Public Art Gallery space in 1910. This photo was taken in 1934.

Attorney Maurice Locke was one of the original trustees of the Dallas Public Library. In 1910 he succeeded Mrs. Exall as president of the board, serving in that position until his death in 1919. (Photo courtesy of Locke, Liddell & Sapp)

the library in size and usefulness to the public." The board elected Miss Wiley librarian at a salary of $1,500 a year.[24]

The services offered by the Dallas Public Library had expanded considerably in recent years. The first branch, Oak Cliff, opened in 1914 (see chapter 3). The library also opened more than a dozen "distribution points" around the city. These varied from a collection of 400 books at Sears Roebuck, paid for by Sears but administered by an assistant from the Main Library who followed a weekly schedule, to small depositories at elementary schools and neighborhood play parks. Other businesses that maintained depositories were the Brown Cracker & Candy Company, Sanger Brothers, and Southwest Telephone and Telegraph Company. The librarian reported in 1917 that a review of the inventory "shows excellent care of the books, considering the use given them, and practically no loss." Employees at these companies seemed to prefer fiction, but "a zealous effort is made to direct the borrower to something better."[25] In the absence of more branch libraries, these depositories represented an effort to make books more easily available to people who might not otherwise visit the Main Library. But they were cumbersome to maintain, and most were gradually phased out by the end of the decade.

The advent of World War I placed additional strains on the library. Demand increased for books, maps, and periodicals relating to military tactics, European geography, and the progress of the war. Housewives sought information on home canning and food conservation. War and adventure stories were popular, as were books about aviation. Circulation increased. "In spite of the war and the many occupations it has imposed upon us all," observed Miss Wiley, "Dallas people are reading more books than ever." The library was even allowing patrons to renew books by telephone. Miss Wiley estimated that during 1918 the library circulated more than 206,000 books. The total collection by now exceeded 60,000 volumes.[26]

The library sold War Savings Stamps and supervised book distribution to servicemen at the new aviation training facility at Love Field and at Camp Dick, an army center at Fair Park. For the first time, the library also allowed advertising and notices of war-related activities to be posted in the reading room.[27] Meanwhile, with able-bodied men at the front, women were enjoying new opportunities in the work force. Well paying government jobs for library-trained individuals were plentiful. With its limited budget, the library was hard pressed to compete for staff. At least ten assistants resigned to take wartime jobs.[28]

Assistant Librarian Betsy Wiley succeeded Rosa Leeper as Librarian in 1916 and served until 1922.

The end of the war brought no relief to the demands on the library. The population of Dallas was nearing 160,000. Dallas was now headquarters for the 12th District of the Federal Reserve and home to Southern Methodist University. The city's new mayor, Frank Wozencraft (a twenty-six-year-old war veteran), asked that library privileges be extended to all Dallas County residents—another 50,000 people—and that branches be established in nearby county towns. The library board declined the request for branches, but it approved extending lending privileges "to all white residents of Dallas County."[29] It also began broadening the scope of its offerings, thanks to the donation by the Wednesday Morning Choral Club of 200 musical recordings. "The experiment of issuing these as we do books will be watched with no little interest," reported Miss Wiley.[30]

The Main Library needed a new roof, better lighting in the reference room, and new window shades. It was again rapidly outgrowing available shelf space. The library also needed a trained librarian for the children's department, especially with the growing national emphasis on raising the standards for children's books. In 1920 the Dallas Public Library began observing Children's Book Week in November. "We regret that its full significance has not impressed all sources that supply juvenile reading," Miss Wiley reported in 1922. "The 'series' idea is still prevalent in some quarters and it is a baneful, melo-dramatic form of recreational reading. Any young person who has been 'fed up' on such a diet is very hard to lead to accept a calmer and better story." The city did spend $5,000 that year in redecorating the interior of the Main Library and installing new light fixtures. But the librarian pointed out that the American Library Association recommended that a community should spend one dollar per person to operate its library each year, while Dallas spent less than eighteen cents.[31]

The responsibilities were becoming too much for Miss Wiley. In May 1920 she submitted her resignation, "for personal reasons." The board persuaded her to withdraw it, but she resigned again in October 1922, and this time the trustees accepted her decision.[32] By now they had an excellent candidate to replace her, Miss Cleora Clanton. Miss Clanton had started work at the Dallas library in 1915 as an unpaid apprentice while waiting to be called for her first teaching job. By the time school began, she was happily entrenched at the library and decided to stay. She worked two years at the main library before spending three years as head of the Oak Cliff branch. She returned downtown in 1921 as assistant to Miss

The Sears Roebuck complex on South Lamar was one of the distribution points maintained by the library during the 1910s as a way of getting books to users who might not venture to the Main Library.

Wiley.[33] Miss Clanton was to direct the Dallas Public Library for the next thirty-two years, longer than any other individual. Miss Leeper and Miss Wiley had guided the library through its first two decades, as it established its place within the community. But the demands on it had grown far beyond the expectations of its founders. It would be left to Miss Clanton to cope with ever increasing space and budgetary problems.

•

The Brown Cracker and Candy Co., in the warehouse district on the northwest side of downtown, was another library distribution point.

(left) Sanger Brothers, the major department store in Dallas, located at Main and Lamar, was yet another library distribution point.

(below) These operators at the Southwestern Telephone & Telegraph building were among other beneficiaries of the library's distribution system in the 1910s.

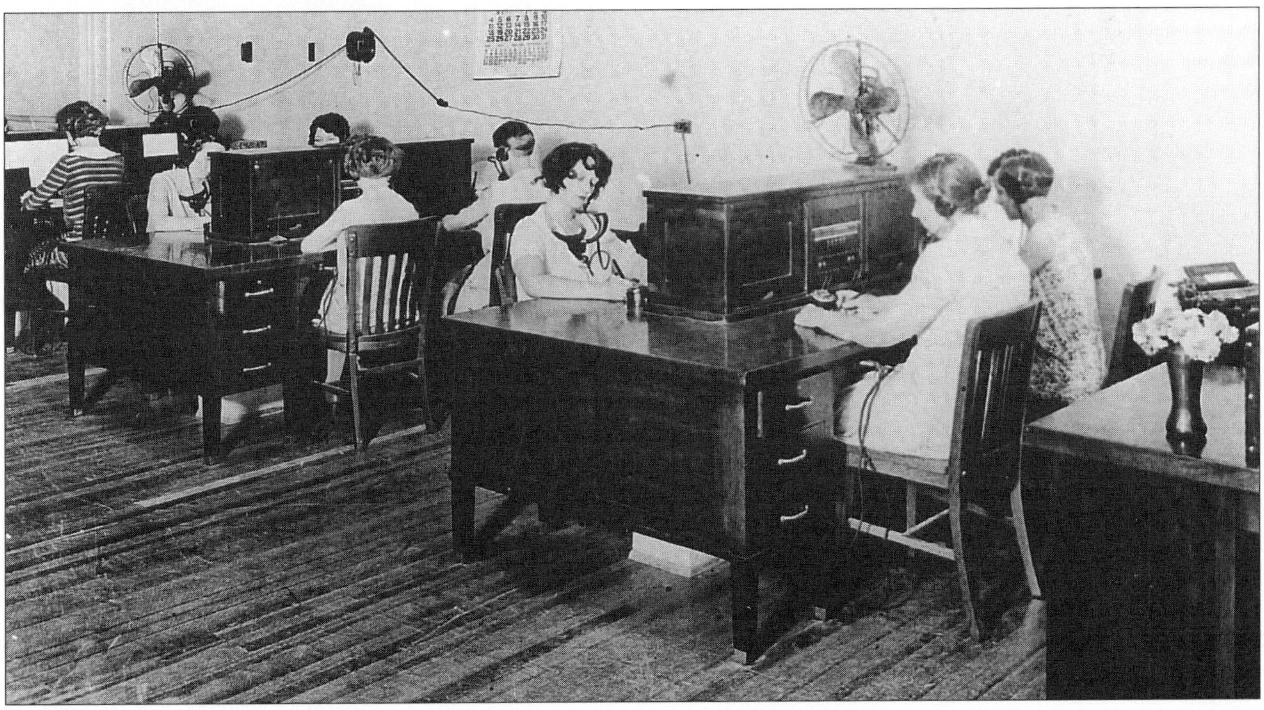

During World War I, the library provided books for soldiers at two training camps in the area.

Frank Wozencraft, a war veteran who became mayor of Dallas while still in his twenties, encouraged the library trustees to expand service throughout Dallas County. (Photo courtesy of the Dallas Municipal Archives)

Camp Dick was one of two military training camps in the Dallas area served by the public library during World War I.

Chapter 3

Branching Out: Oak Cliff

In April 1903 the city of Dallas annexed the neighboring community of Oak Cliff, adding about 4,000 residents to its population. Located west of the Trinity River, the hilly area had attracted settlers almost as early as Dallas. But after it lost an 1850 election for county seat to Dallas, Hord's Ridge, as it was then called, stagnated for several decades. Not until 1887, when real estate speculators began developing the area as a residential suburb called Oak Cliff, and promoting it as "the Brooklyn of Dallas," did significant numbers of people begin to settle there.[1]

By the turn of the century, Oak Cliff boasted its own municipal government, school system, and parks. But the tax base proved inadequate to supply all the necessary city services, and Oak Cliff residents reluctantly voted to allow their town to be annexed by their neighbor across the Trinity. But Oak Cliff retained its unique identity, reinforced by the geographic separation created by the river, whose periodic floods often washed away the bridges and left the community isolated from the rest of Dallas.

When Dallas annexed Oak Cliff, the library trustees approved Miss Leeper's proposal to set up a "delivery station" in Oak Cliff, a place where borrowers could return library books. But

Oak Cliff residents still had to travel several miles into downtown Dallas to use the resources at the library.[2]

Meanwhile the population of Dallas as a whole was growing at a phenomenal rate, far greater than even the most optimistic civic booster would have predicted in 1900. By 1910 the population had more than doubled, to 92,104. The downtown library was finding it increasingly difficult to meet the demands of this growing clientele. A committee of the library board, composed of Mrs. Exall, Maurice Locke, and Alexander Sanger, reported in April 1911 that it was "impossible with present facilities" to give equally efficient service to all parts of the city. "Hundreds of 'want to be' and thousands of 'should be' patrons are kept from using the library by lack of time, and sometimes of carfare as well, necessary to make the trip of two, three, four, and often five miles to the library." The committee had examined reports from similar cities. All showed that branch libraries circulated more than twice the number of volumes, twice as often, at less than half the cost, as the main library. The committee's conclusion was obvious: the most efficient and economical service to a large percentage of the city could be given through branches judiciously distributed. The committee majority (Mrs. Exall and Sanger) recommended that the library board approach Andrew Carnegie for assistance, and that the first branch be built in Oak Cliff. Locke dissented, arguing that the time was not "opportune," but the full board approved the majority recommendation.[3]

Sam Street's Map of Dallas County shows the boundaries in Oak Cliff in 1900.

Almost simultaneously with this action by the library trustees, Mrs. E. B. Reppert, wife

The William Brown Miller family settled west of the Trinity River in 1846 and lived for sixteen years in this log house, which was moved in the 1960s to Old City Park and restored as part of the historical village museum there.

of a local businessman, presented a motion to the Oak Cliff Improvement Society that the society should sponsor a drive to secure a branch library for Oak Cliff. A committee to this end was appointed with Mrs. Reppert as chair, and including such illustrious Oak Cliff residents as Professor W. H. Adamson, principal of Oak Cliff Central School; Mrs. E. P. Turner, one of the first two women elected to the Dallas School Board; and Edward Eisenlohr, a local artist. The committee presented its proposal to the library board in May, with assurances that the residents of Oak Cliff would donate a site.[4]

Maurice Locke, as president of the library board, promptly wrote to Andrew Carnegie on May 13, asking his help in building a branch library in Oak Cliff. Carnegie responded on June 2, "I would be pleased beyond measure to get rid of $25,000, thereby coming a little nearer to the dream of my life—to die poor."[5] His secretary confirmed Carnegie's pledge on June 24, with the provisos that a suitable site be provided and the city of Dallas commit $2,500 per year for maintenance.[6] Carnegie's procedures and qualifications for library grants had become considerably stricter since Dallas obtained its first grant a dozen years ago, and he now required approval of the architectural plans as well.[7] Providing maintenance funds was not a problem, since property taxes were now generating $12,000 annually for the library fund. But approval of the architectural plans would prove to be something of a sticking point.

First, however, the library needed to find a site in Oak Cliff. As soon as Carnegie's support was made known, an Oak Cliff

Library Association was formed with James A. Florer as president. This group agreed to undertake the task of finding a site, and it also agreed to raise $3,000 for books and furniture. The fund-raising goal proved the easier to fulfill. *The Dallas Morning News* published a series of articles about the project, one touting the value of a branch library as a social and cultural center for a community, another arguing that a branch library would encourage home building nearby, and a third citing its educational value for students in the area.[8] By fall the association had the money in the bank. Obtaining a site turned out to be more complicated. The association identified a plot of land owned by the Park Department at the corner of Jefferson Avenue and Marsalis, known as Turner Plaza, as most acceptable. Objections by an adjacent landowner delayed acquisition of the site, and it was not until July 1912 that the land was turned over to the library board.[9]

The developers of Oak Cliff advertised it as the "Brooklyn of Dallas," and many beautiful homes were constructed there in the 1890s, such as these along Ewing Avenue.

That fall, after reviewing a number of bids, the library board selected C. D. Hill & Company to design the building. Their plans specified a one-story stone and steel structure with a basement, covering about eighty by one hundred feet fronting on Jefferson. The architectural plans were displayed at the main library for public comment and then sent to Carnegie's office, as required, in 1913. In December Carnegie's secretary, James Bertram, responded with a number of requests for changes, most notably moving the librarian's desk from a corner of the room to the center for better visibility.[10] Maurice Locke responded promptly that the space on the architectural plans marked "librarian" was really a private office, and that the circulation desk

By the early 1900s several bridges connected the east and west banks of the Trinity River, such as Hutchin's Wagon Bridge, shown here. All were washed away in the flood of 1908.

would indeed be centrally located. He also took the opportunity to review the various provisions made by the city to insure proper maintenance of the facility.[11] Apparently Bertram was satisfied, and Dallas became one of only two cities in Texas to receive a second Carnegie library grant (the other being Houston).

Groundbreaking ceremonies were held March 16, 1914, and a month later the cornerstone was laid, with Dallas Mayor William M. Holland and Library Board Chairman Locke as guest speakers. Inside the stone were placed a variety of articles, including a photograph of Andrew Carnegie, a list of the Oak Cliff citizens prominent in securing the branch library, and newspapers of the day.[12]

Construction continued through the summer and early fall of 1914 with minor delays. The cost was slightly more than the $25,000 provided by Carnegie, but Edward Belsterling, a library trustee, donated fifteen dollars, and $32.41 came from the library's general maintenance fund to make up the difference.[13] The branch opened for service on November 23 under the supervision of Miss Ella Packard, who had worked at the main library for two years after studying in the library training department at the University of Illinois. More than 4,000 books filled the shelves. Some of these had been bought new with the $3,000 raised by the Oak Cliff Library Association, while 214 were loaned by the downtown library. Oak Cliff residents also donated books for the library. Mrs. R. B. Spurgin checked out the first book, *Questions and Answers about Automobiles.*[14]

The first floor of the Oak Cliff Library, as it was officially called, contained a large reading room, a children's room, and the circu-

The Oak Cliff Library, also funded by Andrew Carnegie, opened in 1914 on Jefferson Blvd.

In this photo of the interior of the Oak Cliff Library, the children's room is visible beyond the reading room.

lation desk. The basement contained a 200-seat auditorium for programs such as story hours, as well as for the use of community groups such as mothers' clubs. Naturally, within twenty years the main floor had become so crowded that the children's department was moved to the basement and a storeroom was converted to a teenage reading area.

A fireplace added literal as well as figurative warmth to the children's room.

During its second year of operation, the Oak Cliff library circulated 33,571 books, an increase of 2,000 over the previous year. "After the never ceasing demand for 'Gladiola' and 'Harold-Bell-Wrighteous' fiction," the librarian reported, referring to the "Tarzan" novels, "the classics, sociology, literature, and travel claimed the largest share."[15] By the mid-1920s, Oak Cliff was reporting a circulation of 74,411 volumes, from a collection totaling about 7,000. "This is turning the stacks over more than ten times during the year," reported the librarian—"a splendid argument for branch libraries."[16]

In addition to being the first branch in the Dallas Public Library system, the Oak Cliff Library was also the first to establish a separate children's department and the first to hire a full-time children's librarian.[17] As early as 1917 students from the five Oak Cliff grammar schools were studying thrift, food conservation, and the causes of the war at the library. Saturday morning story hours were attracting about fifty children each week.[18] In 1937 Oak Cliff opened a "Book Nook" for young adults, designed to provide a comfortable transition from children's to adult books. It was stocked with books that had adult appeal but were written in simple language.[19] By the late 1940s Oak Cliff housed more than 30,000 books (about 15,000 of which were in the children's collection), making it the largest branch library. And in June 1952 it achieved the distinction of circulating more books during the month than the main library downtown, nearly 20,000 volumes.[20]

The library was a source of community pride in Oak Cliff, and the *Oak Cliff Tribune* frequently ran feature articles describing its services. But increasingly the stories spoke of overcrowding and understaffing. Structural problems appeared as early as 1927. The Board of Trustees called in Bryan & Sharp, a local architectural firm, to look at the building and was distressed to hear that "the building is in serious condition" and needed "quick action" by the board. However, the city building inspector was less pessimistic, suggesting that some repairs to windows and the roof, as well as removal of the old coal bin, would suffice. The work was done early in 1928, for less than the $1,600 estimate, and "stood the test of the terrific rain storm" not long afterward.[21] The library got a sprucing up in 1950, with new paint, shelves, curtains, and filing cabinets. That year the library installed a photographic charging machine—an innovation for the time—and added shelves, which involved "moving *everything*," reported Ruth Sibley, the librarian. Yet Miss Sibley also found time to write book reviews for the *Oak Cliff Tribune*, conduct a series of six film discussion programs, serve on panels for Lincoln High School and the Texas Library Association, and serve as first vice president of the Oak Cliff Business and Professional Women and co-chairman of the evening section of the Oak Cliff Society of Fine Arts. Her children's librarian spoke to several pre-school PTAs and told stories to groups visiting the library.[22] A group called the Oak Cliff

Students participate in a special program at the Oak Cliff Library about 1933.

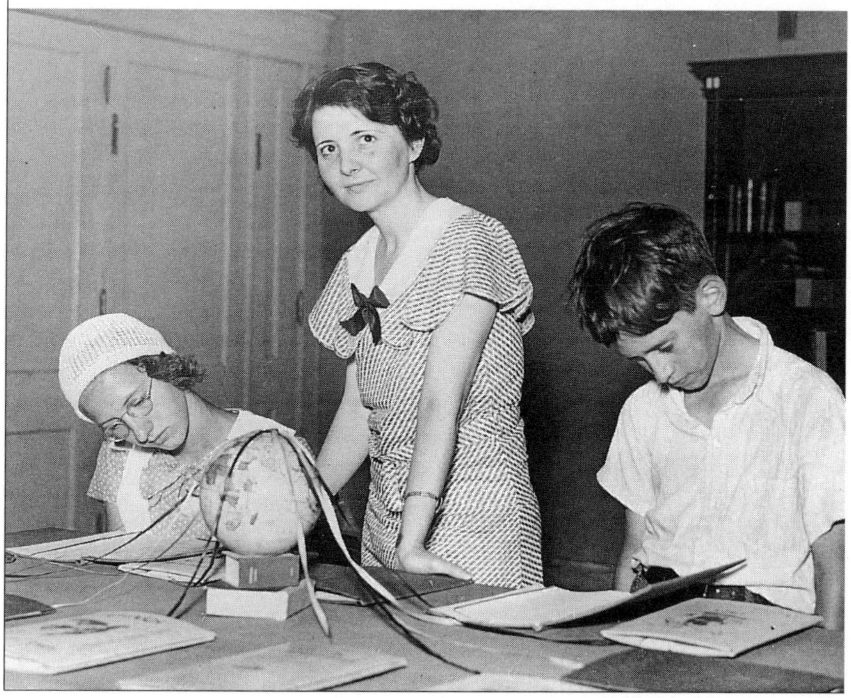

Library Boosters Association raised $7,000 to air condition the library in 1957. And the Oak Cliff Lions Club gave $3,000 to the branch for new books in 1958.[23]

In 1957 Dr. Lowell A. Martin, Dean of the Graduate School of Library Service at Rutgers University, conducted a survey of branch library needs in Dallas. Martin found the Oak Cliff library badly overcrowded. As the collections had grown, the wall bookcases had been supplemented by freestanding cases out in the floor area, which had consumed reading space. There were only three reading tables left on the main floor, and those blocked access to the shelves. Books were stacked on top of the cases, indicating that before long the last of the reading tables would have to go. The space problem, Martin admitted, could be met with an addition to the building. But the problem was more than just an old, overcrowded building. Like the rest of Dallas, Oak Cliff had expanded tremendously in forty years, not only in population but also in geographic area. While 80,000 people lived close to the old city of Oak Cliff in 1950, another 70,000 lived in the broader region west of the Trinity River. Martin pointed out that the population center of Oak Cliff had shifted away from the branch library, and that the neighborhood around it was starting to deteriorate. In his opinion, it would be unwise to invest more money in the present building.[24]

The Oak Cliff Library combined a story hour with a film program in the 1940s.

Martin's report led to a series of bond proposals that funded construction of numerous branch libraries, including one at Hampton-Illinois in Oak Cliff, which opened in 1964. In anticipation of the fact that the 1914 branch would no longer be the

James Robert Faulkner, age nine, found an ideal place to spend a rainy afternoon in 1949—the children's room at the Oak Cliff Library, which had just added 300 new books to its collection.

only one serving Oak Cliff, its name was changed to the Jefferson Avenue Branch. On October 7, 1964, the library board's Evaluation and Development Committee recommended that the old building be replaced rather than repaired. Ground was broken April 5, 1966, just behind the original library, and the new 4,000-square foot branch opened to the public six months later, on October 4. It cost about $105,000.[25] The 1914 structure was then demolished.

The first branch in the Dallas Public Library system, now known as the Jefferson Branch, celebrated its 50th anniversary in November 1964.

The first branch of the Dallas Public Library had survived in its original structure fifty-two years, almost as long as the main branch also funded by Andrew Carnegie. With its community-focused activities, especially its children's programs, the Oak Cliff branch justified the claims of its proponents and established precedents for the branches that followed. While the downtown library remained the center for serious research, the branch library would serve the needs of the children and adults in its surrounding community, collecting books and periodicals of special interest to its users, sponsoring programs to meet their special needs, and providing a site where they could gather. In turn, the community took pride of ownership in the branch library, supporting it with their time and money. It was a mutually beneficial relationship, one that was, in time, to be repeated throughout the city.

•

Construction of a new Jefferson Branch Library began in April 1966. The original building, visible in the rear, was then demolished.

Dallas Mayor J. Erik Jonsson appropriately breaks the ribbon with a book cart at opening ceremonies for the new Jefferson Branch Library on October 4, 1966.

The new Jefferson Branch Library, shown here in 1968, served the area for two decades.

Chapter 4

The Dunbar Branch

Among the assets of Dallas cited by Mrs. Exall in her 1899 request to Andrew Carnegie was the city's racial harmony. "We have never had any race trouble here," she stated. "Our colored population numbers about 8000, and are given exactly the same rights as to voting, justice in the courts, etc., that our white citizens have."[1]

This statement was disingenuous, to say the least. Although racial segregation was not to be legally entrenched in the city's charter until 1907, by the turn of the century African Americans in Dallas were already being confined to distinct neighborhoods and barred from many public facilities. The black community had managed to produce a small professional class of doctors, attorneys, and educators, but most African Americans remained in low-paying occupations. The Dallas public schools were rigidly segregated, and black students had poorer facilities and fewer teachers per pupil than white children. There were no libraries in black schools, because the school board considered the buildings "insecure."[2]

The Board of Trustees of the new Dallas Public Library adhered to the segregationist practices of the time. The second of the "Rules and Regulations" the board approved on July 1, 1901, stated, "Any white person of good deportment, character and habits may use the Reading Rooms." And likewise, Rule No. 6 authorized "All white persons . . . who reside within three and a half miles of the Dallas postoffice" would be entitled to withdraw books.[3]

"Deep Ellum," the stretch of Elm St. adjacent to the Houston & Texas Central Railroad tracks, was a center for African-American music, especially "the blues," during the early twentieth century.

The African-American citizens of Dallas, therefore, were barred from using the public library their tax dollars were helping to support.

Determined to improve literacy and enhance education within their community, in 1906 a number of black leaders raised money, rented a suite of rooms downtown, and furnished them as a library. Apparently they requested assistance from the Dallas Public Library, for a three-member committee of the board responded as follows: "It appears to the Committee, after careful investigation, that the present movement does not have such general support from your people as would justify them in endorsing it. Such action might be construed as taking sides in the question and do more harm than good." The full board approved this letter at its next meeting.[4] After the city charter was amended in 1907 to provide more tax revenue to support the public library, these black leaders wrote the library board again, outlining their efforts and asking that their voluntary library be made a branch of the Carnegie Library.[5] The trustees didn't discuss the letter until the following January, at which time they appointed another committee to study it.[6] There the request died.

In February 1909, the African-American leaders wrote directly to the Carnegie Corporation asking for help. For financial reasons, they had been forced to give up the rented quarters and move the library to Plymouth Congregational Church. They pointed out that Dallas had five grammar schools for black students and one high school, "and in none is there a public reading room or library."[7] Carnegie's secretary, James Bertram, responded, "If the people of Dallas wish a Library building for the colored people, you should have the Mayor and Council write Mr. Carnegie to that effect, stating what they are willing to do in the matter of funds for maintenance."[8]

Two years later Joseph E. Wiley, an African-American entrepreneur who headed the Mill City Cotton Mills, wrote to Bertram, offering to provide a site near the mill and funds to maintain it if Carnegie would help erect the building. Once again Bertram replied that Carnegie could consider only proposals coming from a city's mayor and council.[9]

The Grand Lodge of the Colored Knights of Pythias, comprising many of the African-American professionals in Dallas, tried once more in 1915. Asking Bertram for information on how to apply for assistance, M. M. Rodgers, chairman of the library committee, pointed out, "Of course, the city has a 'Carnegie Public Library,' but it is not open to the colored population."[10] Carnegie's secretary returned his standard reply—that all applications must come from the mayor and city council.

In the past, this had spelled defeat for attempts by the black community to gain support for a library. But the leadership in Dallas had changed with the recent election of Henry D. Lindsley as mayor. A successful businessman who had helped organize the Citizens Association in 1907 to fight for nonpartisan local government, Lindsley was a relatively progressive politician who set up a board of public health, a free legal-aid bureau, and a department of public welfare.[11] He immediately wrote to Carnegie's secretary asking for information. Pointing out that the African-American residents of Dallas

African Americans faced racial segregation even at the State Fair of Texas well into the 1950s, as this advertisement for "Negro Achievement Days" in the Negro City Directory *of 1947-48 indicates.*

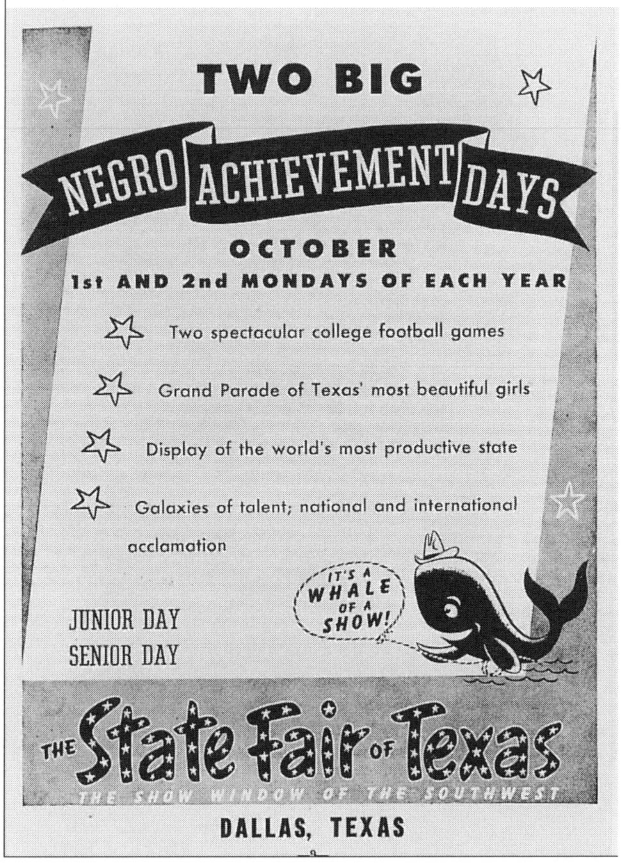

paid taxes on property valued at more than $1.5 million, Lindsley admitted that they received no library privileges. The mayor wrote that he had been assured that a suitable site would be offered, and although the matter had not yet been discussed by the City Commission, he felt confident "that sufficient appropriation of city funds would be arranged to maintain the library along lines similar to the library for white people."[12]

Bertram replied that the mayor "should ascertain the mind of the tax-levying authorities" to confirm that the city would provide $2,500 a year for maintenance if Carnegie granted $25,000 to build a library.[13] Lindsley responded that the city was prepared to provide $2,500 a year for maintenance and that the Dallas Public Library Association would supervise the new facility. He had also received assurances from leaders in the African-American community that they would provide a suitable lot and contribute $2,500 toward equipping the library.[14]

At last the long struggle to build a library for Dallas's African-American residents seemed to be nearing success. The city's black and white leadership had finally united in formulating an appeal that appeared to meet Carnegie's requirements. One can only imagine, then, the frustration all parties must have felt when Bertram wrote to Lindsley in June announcing that, because of the poor record of Texas libraries in fulfilling their pledges, "the Board of Trustees of this Corporation have been led to suspend for the present the giving of such library buildings in the State of Texas."[15]

In his response, Lindsley pointed out that the city of Dallas had "in every way" kept its pledges to Carnegie, and he respectfully suggested that Dallas "should be considered on its own mer-

Rule #2 of the Dallas Public Library, formulated in 1901, clearly restricted use of the library to "white persons," thereby barring African-American citizens from using the facility.

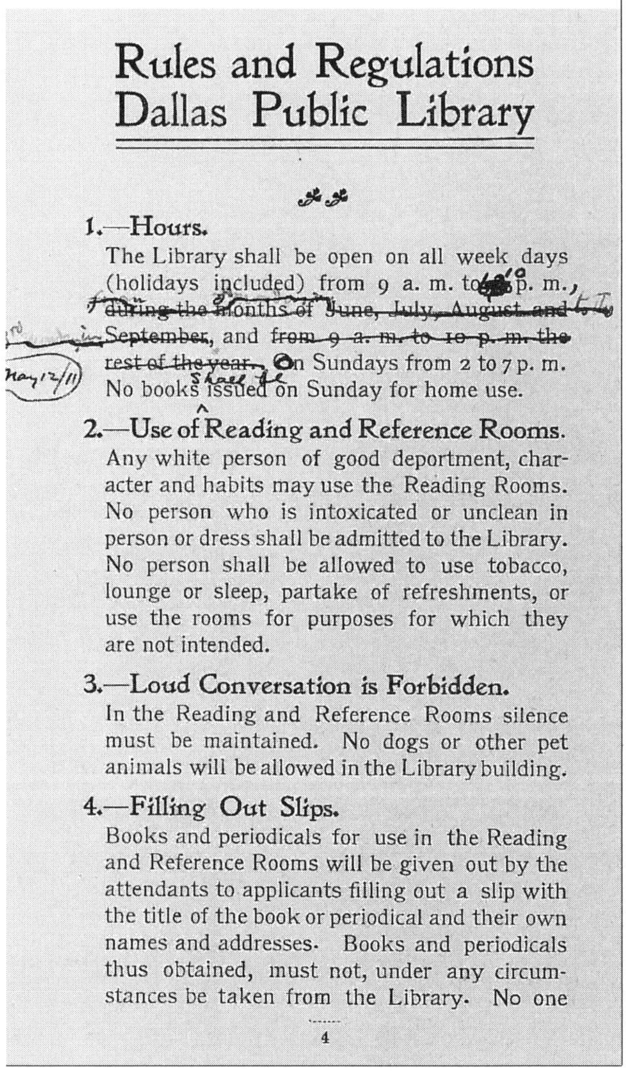

Rules and Regulations
Dallas Public Library

1.—Hours.
The Library shall be open on all week days (holidays included) from 9 a. m. to 10 p. m., during the months of June, July, August and September, and from 9 a. m. to 10 p. m. the rest of the year. On Sundays from 2 to 7 p. m. No books issued on Sunday for home use.

2.—Use of Reading and Reference Rooms.
Any white person of good deportment, character and habits may use the Reading Rooms. No person who is intoxicated or unclean in person or dress shall be admitted to the Library. No person shall be allowed to use tobacco, lounge or sleep, partake of refreshments, or use the rooms for purposes for which they are not intended.

3.—Loud Conversation is Forbidden.
In the Reading and Reference Rooms silence must be maintained. No dogs or other pet animals will be allowed in the Library building.

4.—Filling Out Slips.
Books and periodicals for use in the Reading and Reference Rooms will be given out by the attendants to applicants filling out a slip with the title of the book or periodical and their own names and addresses. Books and periodicals thus obtained, must not, under any circumstances be taken from the Library. No one

4

Mayor Henry D. Lindsley supported efforts in 1915 to obtain Carnegie support for a library serving African Americans in Dallas. (Photo courtesy of the Dallas Municipal Archives)

its, and should not be placed with other cities, whether in Texas or elsewhere, which may have failed to keep their pledges to the Carnegie Corporation."[16] After receiving a rather lame reply from Bertram, suggesting that perhaps the mayor should use his influence to encourage the delinquent Texas towns to fulfill their pledges, Lindsley wrote another, sharper letter, arguing that the corporation's position was "utterly inconsistent with a correct conception of this matter," and asking Bertram to read the entire correspondence to the board.[17]

Here the matter ended, and in 1917 the Carnegie Corporation terminated funding for all new libraries and began turning its attention to endowing library schools, assisting the Library of Congress, and finding ways to bring books to people in rural areas.[18] The initiative to build a library for African Americans in Dallas (at least with Carnegie support) was the victim, to some extent, of unlucky timing.

Educators, both black and white, continued to be especially concerned over the deprivation of books to African-American children. As early as 1910 the school district had worked out an arrangement with the public library to borrow books for use by teachers at what was then called the Colored High School. Two years later Miss Leeper reported that a number of books at the school had been lost during the summer vacation, and she asked for guidance. On a motion by Mrs. W. A. Calloway (who, in her newspaper column under the penname "Pauline Periwinkle," was a staunch supporter of progressive reforms), seconded by Mrs. Exall, Miss Leeper was instructed to continue the service and to replenish the library with suitable books.[19] In 1916 Superintendent Justin Kimball appealed for more books for African-American citizens, but the library board deferred action. The school board tried again in 1921, suggesting that Booker T. Washington High School, then under construction, might provide "proper housing" for a library. Again the trustees deferred action.[20]

The next few years represented a low point in race relations in Dallas, as the Ku Klux Klan gained a foothold in local government. Attacks on African Americans, Catholics, and Jews went almost unpunished, while 160,000 people turned out for KKK Day at the State Fair in 1923. Only with the defeat of Klan candidate Felix Robertson for Governor in 1926, and revelations of Klan outrages around the country, did the Klan's influence begin to wane.[21] But the effort to secure a library for black citizens was put on hold.

As the main library downtown began to suffer from overcrowding, the sentiment in favor of establishing branches began to grow. In 1925 the mayor appointed a committee chaired by businessman Charles E. Ulrickson to update the city's master plan for development. Among the proposals of the Ulrickson Report, as it was dubbed, was the addition of four branch libraries, including one for the city's African-American residents.[22] Cleora Clanton, head librarian, strongly supported this recommendation. "We owe this to them as American citizens," she told the library trustees, "regardless of any stand on the race question."[23] In December 1927 voters approved a $23.9 million bond package that included $500,000 for the libraries, as well as an addition of one cent on the tax base for library support.

The Colored High School, at Hall and Cochran streets, served all African-American students in Dallas County from 1892 to 1922. Because it had no library, and African-American students were barred from using the public library, library trustees arranged to deposit some books at the school.

With funding available, the library board began planning branch libraries for both black citizens and the mostly Jewish residents of South Dallas. At a meeting in June 1928, the Board authorized one of its members, Edward Belsterling, to negotiate with black leaders for a site in the neighborhood of Booker T. Washington High School. Much like the Carnegie Corporation, the library board expected members of the community, the future users of the branch library, to take an active role in building their library, from helping select and provide a site to raising funds for equipment. At the request of Professor J. J. Rhoades, principal of Booker T. Washington High School, the board appointed a committee of black citizens, chaired by Dr. J. W. Anderson, to head the fund-raising campaign within the African-American community. The Colored Teachers' State Association of Texas pledged $1,000, and students at the four Dallas elementary schools serving African Americans raised $144.10.[24] After protracted negotiations, the board voted to purchase a site at the corner of Thomas and Worthington for $8,000 and awarded construction contracts totaling more than $20,000.[25]

The library site was in the heart of the area known as "North Dallas" within the African-American community. This neighborhood had grown up around the original Freedman's Town, established by former slaves following the Civil War. Here were located the homes and businesses of prominent African Americans, as well as churches and the only medical facilities where black physicians could practice. The library was a few blocks north of Booker T. Washington High School, which served all black high school students in Dallas County.

Booker T. Washington High School opened in 1922 on Flora Street, replacing the old Colored High School.

In February 1931, the board formally approved naming the new branch library for Paul Laurence Dunbar, the distinguished African-American poet. The architects Ralph B. Bryan and Walter P. Sharp, who had also designed the nearby Moorland Branch Y.M.C.A., planned an L-

During the 1920s Dallas was a hot bed for the Ku Klux Klan, boasting the largest enrollment of any community in the nation.

shaped brick building, with high ceilings and tall casement windows. A massive fireplace in the children's bay was the principal interior feature. To head the library, the board hired Mrs. Alma Deere Venters, described by Miss Clanton as "a native Texan of splendid reputation, and having had more library training and experience than any who were found to be available." Mrs. Venters had earned a B.S. degree from Paul Quinn College and an A. B. from Sam Houston College, and she had trained in library work in both these schools and in Hampton Institute, Virginia.[26]

The opening of the Dunbar branch library on June 29, 1931, was a cause of great celebration. Representatives of all the schools serving African-American students in Dallas took part in a reception and "inspection," as did members of the Ladies Reading Circle and the YWCA. They found 2,000 books on the shelves, purchased for about $4,500, many of them by African-American authors.[27] A photograph in the leading black newspaper was, appropriately, entitled "A Dream Come True."

Within five years, Mrs. Venters had built the collection to some 6,000 volumes (some purchased with the money raised by African-American school children), and more than 3,300 readers held library cards. The Dunbar branch sponsored forum and discussion groups and presented noted speakers. "In her quiet and effective way," observed the *Dallas Express*, "without show or bluster, the library has been developed as a center of racial culture with special emphasis on the inculcation of reading habits among the children of the community."[28] The branch celebrated National Book Week each November with programs produced by elementary school children, and during the summer it spon-

The Paul Laurence Dunbar Branch of the Dallas Public Library stood at the corner of Thomas and Worthington streets in the heart of Dallas's original Freedman's Town neighborhood.

Eager patrons flood the Dunbar Branch for its dedication, June 29, 1931.

The children's room occupied one wing of the Dunbar Branch.

sored reading clubs. During 1937 Mrs. Venters wrote a regular column for the *Informer*, an African-American newspaper, calling attention to noteworthy books.

Circulation reached 18,000 volumes during 1937. A reporter for the *Dallas Times Herald* attributed the heavy use of the Dunbar library to the fact that many of its patrons lived in crowded quarters without the privacy needed for reading. As a result, African Americans used the library "in a larger proportion than white people."[29] So busy did the Dunbar branch become that in 1938 officials of the Negro Chamber of Commerce contacted the library board asking that three assistants be appointed. Currently, they noted, Mrs. Venters was running the library by herself, and the facility was open only from 1 to 8 p.m., causing inconvenience for both children and adults who might want to use it during the morning.[30] A year later, still without help, Mrs. Venters resigned to become librarian at the new Lincoln High School.

Mrs. Venters' resignation was greeted with understandable concern, especially when the Dunbar branch was forced to cut back its hours for a time, but her replacement, Lemmon McMillan, was welcomed with pride as a Dallas native who had graduated from Booker T. Washington High School, earned a degree from Prairie View College, and trained at the main Dallas library downtown. "He is winning the confidence of the public," reported the *Dallas Gazette*, "stimulating a desire for better reading and meriting a success in his work that any one could be proud of."[31] Under McMillan's direction, in April 1940 Dunbar checked out

The reference and reading room occupied another wing of the Dunbar Branch.

A group of costumed children celebrate National Book Week at the Dunbar Branch in November 1949.

2,000 books in one month.[32] That month the Beta Delta Chapter of Delta Sigma Theta Sorority offered to fund, on an annual basis, the purchase of books on Negro life and culture for the library, an offer the library gratefully accepted.[33]

But in the years following World War II, the neighborhood around the Dunbar branch underwent dramatic changes, not unlike those that affected the Oak Cliff branch. The construction of Central Expressway displaced many residents and sliced through the neighborhood. The remaining dwellings were aging, and commercial development was encroaching. Many families with children began moving to South and West Dallas and, after 1954, into Hamilton Park, a new, middle-class African-American neighborhood in far North Dallas.

The circulation of books at the Dunbar branch lagged. A library committee that studied the problem concluded that the books in the branch were outdated and too limited in subject matter. The branch was also inconveniently located for most of its users and was not open during optimum hours.[34] African Americans had been able to use the downtown library, at least on a limited basis, since the 1940s.[35] Once the new Central Library opened in 1955, they had free access to all its resources. (See Chapter 7.) In his survey of branch libraries, issued in January 1958, Dr. Lowell Martin concurred that the Dunbar branch, along with Oak Cliff and two of the other branches, was too close to downtown Dallas. New branches, he recommended, should be built farther out, preferably in shopping centers that attracted large numbers of people. He also pointedly recommended that all the branches should be open to all users, regardless of race.[36]

Acting on Martin's advice, the library board planned a new branch in West Dallas, designed to serve the mostly African-American residents of that area. And in May 1959, the trustees voted to close and sell Dunbar.[37] Built in response to the institutionalized racism of the early twentieth century, it had served its community as best it could with limited resources. But by the late 1950s, its time had clearly passed.[38]

Mrs. Willetta McGaskey and her second-grade class from J. W. Ray Elementary School participate in story time at the Dunbar Branch in 1948.

The construction of Central Expressway along the old Houston & Texas Central Railroad right-of-way after World War II bisected the African-American neighborhood served by the Dunbar Branch and promoted a decline in usage.

Chapter 5
The Clanton Administration

Almost as soon as Cleora Clanton became Librarian in 1922, she was faced with a financial crisis. The tax revenue provided by the city was running out. One of the newspapers quoted Miss Clanton as warning that the library had only enough money to keep operating until October and that there were no funds at all for the Oak Cliff branch.[1] Somehow, the library stayed open, and early in 1924 officials voted $10,000 in additional funds to avert the crisis. But the current tax rate of one and a half cents per one hundred dollars valuation was clearly inadequate to sustain the library's operations. This worked out to about sixteen cents per citizen, "a smaller sum than a man would offer as a tip to the waitress for handing him a cup of coffee and a sandwich," observed Miss Clanton.[2] As a result, Dallas was falling behind. Miss Clanton pointed out in 1926 that Houston was spending twice what Dallas did on new books.[3]

Equally serious was the rapid deterioration of the main library building. "The fountains haven't worked in years," Miss Clanton reported to the board in 1923. "Plaster is cracking, even falling in many places."[4] As the library approached its twenty-fifth anniversary in 1926, a local newspaper reported that an employee had to drop a handful of books to jump aside when several square feet of ceiling tumbled down.[5] W. T. Henry, president of the library board, declared that the walls were crumbling, and unless they were repaired, the structure would be unsafe.[6]

The library was becoming seriously overcrowded. By the early 1920s, the main library contained 60,000 volumes, six times its initial holdings. Yet, according to Miss Clanton, the library really needed $25,000 worth of new books. "If all the books which are worn out and dirty from constant use were withdrawn, hundreds would be taken from the shelves," she reported to the trustees. "Because of their great popularity and the library's inability to duplicate for lack of funds, many of these have been retained even though the book is little more than a rag."[7] Use of the library was growing steadily. A thousand books were checked out on a typical day downtown, and another 200 in Oak Cliff; some days the totals reached 2,000.[8] Yet Miss Clanton felt the circulation could double if the library had the needed resources, "for it takes as much time and money to report to a patron that a book is not available as it would to give him the book, and it is not nearly so satisfactory to him or to us."[9]

Cleora Clanton, shown here in 1951, headed the Dallas Public Library for thirty-two years, longer than any other director.

Miss Clanton was particularly proud of the services provided in the reference room. "You'll find every table crowded and every chair taken, with generally an impatient line," she told a reporter in 1926."[10] Here, businessmen, researchers, and professional writers had access to the information they needed. The Dallas Public Library was a depository for U.S. Government publications, including books, maps, magazines, pamphlets, and bulletins. The government reports "have become so popular and so scarce," Miss Clanton reported, "that the library uses every precaution except chaining them to the shelves to keep them intact."[11] On some days, people were observed leaning against the walls waiting for someone to vacate a chair. "It is an outrage,"

By 1942, when this photograph of the circulation desk was taken, the Main Library was overcrowded and suffering from years of inadequate maintenance.

The Alexander Sanger Branch Library opened in 1932 at the intersection of Park Row and Harwood.

This view inside the Sanger Library looks past the circulation desk toward the children's area.

exclaimed Miss Clanton, "when people who are in earnest about seeking information have to play pussy-wants-a-corner in order to obtain a portion of a table in the library."[12]

Early in 1927 the library trustees called for an increase from one and a half cents to three cents per one hundred dollars property valuation for maintenance and operation of the library. They estimated that this increase would provide about $65,000 per year. "The library is simply starving to death for want of money," observed Boude Storey, one of the trustees. The increase would have required an amendment to the city charter, which Mayor Louis Blaylock opposed. The library board therefore withdrew its petition and asked instead that library funding be included in a bond proposal being planned for later in the year.[13] The bond package approved by voters in December did raise the tax rate by a penny, and it included $500,000 for the library, mostly for neighborhood branches. The librarians were jubilant. "Citizens put their stamp of approval on this institution," wrote Miss Clanton in her annual report to the trustees. "While the funds are not actually available, we know they will be, and this gives impetus to better service."[14]

The prospect of obtaining a branch library excited people in various parts of the city. The residents of South Dallas notified the board that they were interested in having the first branch funded through the bond sales and were prepared to provide a site. Because of the presence of several synagogues, South Dallas was home to most of Dallas's Jewish population, including "merchant princes" such as the Sangers, Marcuses, and Kahns. These families had always supported the library and recognized the ben-

The library opened a depository collection of children's books in the Sam Houston Elementary School in 1929. A year later the facility moved into rented quarters nearby as the Oak Lawn Branch Library.

efit, especially to their children, of having a branch located in their neighborhood. The library board authorized one of its members, Milton Hickox, to negotiate with the South Dallas leaders for a lot. Much like the experience in Oak Cliff, finding a suitable site at a reasonable price proved more difficult than expected, and it wasn't until February 1930 that the board voted to buy property at the northwest corner of Harwood and Park Row, for not more than $7,500, for the South Dallas branch.[15]

Dallas architect Henry Coke Knight was retained to design the branch library. He planned a red brick structure, of contemporary French influence, with a slate mansard roof and an entrance of natural stone. When South Dallas residents protested the fact that Coke's plans faced the building on Harwood rather than Park Row, the board instructed him to meet with them to resolve the matter.[16] The parties compromised, and the entrance was placed at an angle, facing the corner. Construction proceeded during 1931, and the branch officially opened on February 1, 1932. The board voted to name it the Alexander Sanger Branch, in honor of one of the early supporters of the Dallas Public Library who had also been a resident of South Dallas. The Sanger Branch opened with 3,000 volumes and cost nearly $45,000.[17]

The first of the bonds approved by voters in the December 1927 election came up for sale late in 1929, on the eve of the stock market crash and the onset of the Great Depression. The funds from this first sale were used to build the Dunbar and Sanger branches. But the subsequent planned bond sales were postponed

The East Dallas Branch Library opened in 1938 in this building, which once housed an ice cream parlor.

indefinitely, and the library's schedule for repairing the central building and constructing four new branch libraries was disrupted. In 1930 the library did open a small branch in a rented building in Oak Lawn, the neighborhood north of downtown. This replaced a branch in the Sam Houston Elementary School, which opened a year earlier with 1,200 books. Originally the Oak Lawn branch was intended to serve only children, but so many adults asked for service that several hundred adult books were added to the collection.[18] And in 1937 the library bought an existing building in East Dallas, formerly occupied by a Cabell's ice cream parlor, and converted it into a branch for the residents of the developing Lakewood neighborhood as well as Junius Heights, Munger Place, and other East Dallas areas.

Residents of Lakewood and other East Dallas neighborhoods kept the small library a busy place.

The East Dallas branch opened on January 3, 1938, staffed by two librarians, Marion Underwood and Mary Rice. Mrs. Underwood was a registered nurse with a degree from Johns Hopkins University who had also taken some library training. She had worked as the children's librarian downtown before Cleora Clanton asked her to head the new East Dallas branch. She supervised the branch for three decades, becoming a beloved neighborhood figure. "We were very informal," she recalled in a 1973 interview. "We took down the 'Quiet' signs and let people smoke . . . We were always interested in people's illnesses and their love affairs and their marriages and their children." Once the library hosted a party for dogs during National Dog Week. "We had about eight dogs," Mrs. Underwood remembered. "It was a rainy day, very muddy; they tracked mud in, but they behaved themselves. I served ice cream and puppy biscuits."

Like dedicated librarians downtown and at the other branches, Mrs. Underwood did whatever needed to be done to keep the library going. One day the janitor didn't show up. "It was hot, hot, hot. Before air conditioning," recalled Mrs. Underwood. "So I took off my dress and pulled the blinds, got the mop out and mopped the floor." She had to cope with the unpredictable. On another occasion, a golf ball came through the bay window and landed on her desk, soon retrieved by an elderly man playing at the Lakewood Country Club course across the street.[19] Like the other neighborhood branches, East Dallas became a community center, the place where mothers brought their toddlers for story hour, where children came after school to study and do research, and where older folks met friendly faces while checking out the latest books and periodicals.

Cleora Clanton, center, joins Marion Underwood, head of the East Dallas Branch, and Mary Rice, Underwood's assistant, in celebrating the branch's tenth anniversary in 1948.

The Great Depression that hit the nation at the end of 1929 had put 18,500 Dallasites out of work by 1931. Library usage increased dramatically, as the unemployed found themselves with time on their hands, and the populace in general sought inexpensive ways to fill their leisure time. Circulation more than doubled between 1930 and 1933, reaching nearly a million. "The insecurity and uncertainty of the last five years have sent thousands of men and women to the library who had never before thought of entering its doors," Miss Clanton reported to the trustees in 1934. "Books covering every phase of human endeavor have been in demand, but most interesting is the fact that books on economics and government which have stood on the shelves as faithfully as the tin soldier of Little Boy Blue fame and almost as dusty, have been taken out, aired, dusted, and actually read."[20]

By the early 1930s, more than 100,000 Dallasites had borrowers cards, out of a total population of about 250,000. The library's income declined fifteen percent in 1933, but it was still able to add 10,000 books to the collections.[21] It did benefit in 1935 from the assignment of eight women from the Works Progress Administration, who assisted in cataloguing, updating the clipping and pamphlet files, and mending and binding.[22] In 1936 it reached out to a new audience by acquiring its first talking book for the blind machine; records could be borrowed free from the State Library.[23] And in 1939, "after making a thorough investigation of the use of microfilm and reading machines," the library invested in an Argus reader. "Microfilm is revolutionizing research," Miss Clanton explained, "as it is making it possible to bring rare and scarce material to any scholar anywhere there is a microfilm reader."[24] The staff became increasingly creative about finding space. When the library changed from coal heating to a gas furnace, the old coal bin in the basement was converted into the magazine and newspaper reading room.[25] "This is the last move that can be made to give more space," Miss Clanton warned the trustees, "as every available area has now been utilized."[26]

John William Rogers, arts critic for the *Dallas Times*

This aerial photograph shows the East Dallas Library strategically located next to the Lakewood Shopping Center, adjacent to residential neighborhoods, and across from the Lakewood Country Club golf course.

In 1952 Cleora Clanton was photographed holding a bucket to catch leaks in the roof of the Main Library, graphically illustrating the serious structural problems with the old building.

In 1939 the library established a Reader's Advisory Service to provide additional services to patrons. When this photograph was taken in 1942, it was doubling as the War Information Center.

Herald, wrote a long article about the library in 1937, pointing out that Dallas had the lowest per capita expenditure on library services of any city in the country with a population over 200,000 except for New Orleans and Houston. Yet its organization was so efficient, that its cost per book issued—a little less then ten cents—was the lowest in the United States. Miss Clanton told Rogers that nonfiction now constituted forty percent of the library's circulation, a development she attributed to readers' growing interest in self-improvement. "With pardonable pride," she attributed this shift toward more serious reading to the role libraries had played in adult education.

Rogers asked Miss Clanton what improvements she would like to see in the Dallas library—setting aside for the moment such practical issues as cost. First, she said, would be a new central library with proper climate control, not only for the comfort of patrons and staff, but also for preservation of the collection. The new library would include specialized rooms devoted to art, music, and business, with trained personnel to staff them. A readers' advisory service would develop educational programs to meet individual needs. "The goal of public libraries should be more than the quantity of books borrowed," Miss Clanton explained. "It should take into account the kind of books read and to what purpose."[27]

Miss Clanton began several of her annual reports during the 1930s with the same paragraph: "Probably no institution in the city touches the lives of the citizens at more points than the Public Library. Scarcely any project or endeavor continues long without requiring its assistance. The extent of its value is limited only by the extent of its resources, which in turn depend on its financial support."[28] Miss Clanton and the library board knew what they needed, but in the late 1930s Dallas lacked both the money and the momentum to achieve their goals. Meanwhile, the central library continued to deteriorate. Only the most critical repairs were made. In 1938 the *Dallas Times Herald* published a photograph of scaffolding covering the front of the building while workmen patched stones in danger of falling and tried to fix leaks in the roof.[29] In the summer of 1941 much of the second floor was deemed unsafe, and all the books except those in the children's section were removed.[30] Reinforcement of the floor was scheduled to start in October, but until then the reference department and periodicals reading room were closed.[31] Miss Clanton was photographed in the furnace room, where reference books, both loose and boxed, had been stored; boxes of books also crowded the aisles in the first floor stacks.[32] But the librarian remained positive. "While its physical appearance and ability to function have suffered during the years," she observed, "its heart is still sound and its spirit unbroken."[33]

Bertha Landers (left) headed the Visual Education Department, which began during World War II with war-related films and continued to expand after the war.

In 1941, on the eve of America's entry into World War II, the Dallas Public Library circulated 822,572 books. More than 90,000 persons were registered borrowers, 35,000 of these children under age eighteen. The war created new demands on the library. Reading habits again altered, with renewed interest in technical literature, and pamphlets on home gardening and food preservation. The library established a "War and Local Defense Information" desk with the latest facts, reports, directives, regulations, and instructions. As it had done during World War I, the library board

Siddie Joe Johnson, shown here in the children's room of the Main Library about 1944, headed the children's department for nearly thirty years, developing a host of programs that encouraged a love of books and reading in Dallas youngsters.

relaxed its ban on advertising material in the library, allowing recruiting posters and civilian defense material to be posted. The library also made books available to servicemen stationed at the various bases around Dallas, as well as at the train station and the USOs. In 1942 the Dallas Public Library became the first public library to be designated a Government War Film Depository. With 16 mm. films supplied by the armed forces and the Federal government, the library established a Visual Education Department. Many of these films were produced to acquaint civilians with gasoline rationing, scrap metal salvage, and similar projects.[34] Headed by Bertha Landers, the Visual Education Department continued to develop after the war, becoming one of the nation's best and leading the "film" revolution from books to video.

Despite the special services necessitated by the war, the library continued to develop programs for its normal constituencies, particularly children. Since its opening, of course, the library had devoted space and resources to its children's collection, and by the early 1930s it was sponsoring vacation reading clubs, craft and hobby shows, and special exhibits during National Children's Book Week.[35] But the children's programs took on a new life in 1937 with the hiring of Siddie Joe Johnson as children's librarian. A graduate of Texas Christian University in Fort Worth, Miss Johnson taught school for a year. "Then I rediscovered children's books and knew that was it." She earned a master's degree in library science from Louisiana State University and headed the Corpus Christi library before coming to Dallas. When she asked about starting a creative program to encourage children's reading, she was discouraged. "They told me to forget about story hours. There wouldn't be enough interest. We held one anyway. It rained that day, and only five bedraggled children were there. But it was a start." Eventually as many as 300 children packed the Saturday morning programs. Miss Johnson also taught creative writing classes on Friday afternoons and gained national prominence as an author of children's books. She served as juvenile editor of the book page for *The Dallas Morning News* for twenty-seven years and conducted a weekly radio program.[36] In 1954 she became the first recipient of the Grolier Society award for achievement as a children's librarian.[37] During her nearly three decades at the Dallas Public Library, she helped develop a love of books and reading in thousands of children.

A group of children attend a story hour and film program on Mexican Children and the Arts and Crafts of Mexico in 1948.

The war did take a toll on the library. Budgets were very tight, forcing some staff cutbacks. The branches were especially hard hit. At the Sanger branch, for instance, Mrs. Elizabeth Scott, the manager, was the only full-time employee, assisted by Tom Bogie, a high school student who worked after school and on weekends. On at least one Saturday, when Mrs. Scott had to be out of town, Bogie was left to open and close the library by himself. Violet Hayden, the assistant librarian, ordered all the adult books for the entire system, while Siddie Joe Johnson selected the children's books. The budget was barely adequate to acquire the most popular, current books, and the supply coming to Sanger was so small, Bogie later recalled, that a porter could bring them, along with other supplies, in a parcel on the streetcar. As a result, circulation began to decline at Sanger, as neighborhood patrons traveled the extra mile downtown to the Main Library, where the selection was wider.[38]

With the end of the war, the library renewed its campaign for a new central building. The *Dallas Times Herald* helped by publishing an article under the headline, "Dallas Library So Crowded Books Stored in Boiler Room." The reporter described "shelves bulging with books, inadequate help, not enough catalog space, not enough floor or shelf space." The annual appropriation of

$73,100 ran and equipped a library that boasted the largest circulation of any in Texas. The staff now numbered twenty-eight full-time assistants, but some of these were at the branch libraries.[39] The city was currently developing another city plan, drawn up by Harland Bartholomew, a national consultant. The present central library, Bartholomew concluded, "has outlived its usefulness and is now inadequate to serve existing needs." He recommended a new, three-story building containing at least 60,000 square feet of floor space. Bartholomew's recommendations resulted in a bond proposal, which won voter approval, and which included $1 million for a new central library. Since $300,000 still remained from the 1927 bond issue, the library, in theory, would have $1.3 million to work with. But like the earlier issue, the question remained, when would the bonds be sold and the funds become available?

By the time of her retirement in 1965, Siddie Joe Johnson had earned national recognition for her outstanding work as a children's librarian.

Nothing had happened by the beginning of 1948, when *The Dallas Morning News* ran an article under the headline, "Dallas Has Worst Library for U.S. Cities of Its Size." Even more graphically than earlier accounts, this article described the deplorable conditions in the downtown library. It also calculated that the current budget worked out to thirty-six cents per citizen, while the American Library Association's minimal goal for library service in any city with a population between 300,000 and 500,000 was one dollar.[40] The article sparked some not too amusing controversy, when Oklahoma City disputed Dallas's claim to having the worst library, saying that it spent only thirty-two cents per resident. Hughes Springs, Texas, responded that it didn't have a library at all.[41] But the publicity did instigate a tour of the library by the City Council. Afterwards, Mayor Jimmie Temple described it as a "booby trap." "This building isn't old," he exclaimed. "It's ancient."[42] The City Council granted the library board's request for $20,000 in emergency funds for repairs, supplies, and salary increases.

Thousands of new residents were moving to Dallas in the post-war era, often from cities with much better supported libraries. Cleora Clanton was savvy enough to recognize that their influence on city councilmen and library trustees could be helpful. In 1939 she had created a new department, Readers Advisory Service, which prepared individual study courses for patrons and publicized library services through printed book lists, displays, and contact with civic organizations.[43] The service had become dormant during the war, but in 1947 Miss Clanton appointed a new staff member, Lillian Moore Bradshaw, to head it. Despite some aspirations to a stage career, Mrs. Bradshaw earned degrees at Western Maryland College and Drexel University and worked at the public library in Utica, New York, and the Enoch Pratt Free Library in Baltimore before moving to Dallas. After a brief stint heading the Sanger Branch, she was called to the central library to develop the Readers Advisory Service, which was essentially a public relations project. "I was supposed to go out and make speeches to the new clubs growing up in Dallas," she recalled. She helped plan their programs and organized study clubs, in the process cultivating loyal supporters for the library.[44]

Another successful outreach program of the post-war period was the bookmobile. Funded by the Dallas Federation of Women's Clubs in 1949, the library-on-wheels held about 1,800 books and stopped at a different neighborhood each day. The bookmobile proved enormously popular. One afternoon it made a scheduled stop in a drenching downpour. The librarian expected to be alone all day. To her surprise, forty people were waiting in the rain, and within two hours, 175 patrons had checked out books. On some days, the bookmobile issued 600 books in three hours.[45]

The Dallas Federation of Women's Clubs donated the first bookmobile to the Dallas Public Library in 1949.

But bookmobiles were stopgap measures, designed to try to meet the pressing need for more branch libraries. The library board was growing increasingly frustrated with the lack of city support. It threatened to close the library one or two months each year unless its tax revenues were increased, but the City Council refused to submit a charter amendment to that effect.[46] It considered charging fees for nonresidents of Dallas, but the mayors of towns throughout Dallas County protested, and the board backed off.[47]

By midcentury the Dallas Public Library was circulating about 700,000 books, but Cleora Clanton pointed out that this was well below the American Library Association's recommendations for a city the size of Dallas, whose population had reached 434,000. The library should be circulating two million books a year. The problem, of course, was lack of funds. "You can not circulate books which you do not have, nor can you expect people to travel long distances to be told that the books they need are not available," Miss Clanton warned. "We need more, many more books, and we need branches to make the books more easily available, which in turn means more personnel."[48]

In her first annual report to the board, Cleora Clanton had mentioned the library's need for more money. "The refrain became the library theme song," she wrote in 1947, "and has been featured in every monthly and annual report since that time. Sometimes the librarian sings it as a solo, sometimes there are variations with the Board joining in, sort of a la Fred Waring, sometimes the patrons and citizens join in in a kind of Billy Sunday revival with the newspapers taking top line. Once in a while the city fathers add a few dollars to the budget and kind citizens drop a few dollars in the cup, but by and large no one seems to be too impressed." All of which meant, she concluded, "that we shall continue with the same theme until Dallas has a building and a budget commensurate with its needs."[49]

As the Dallas Public Library approached its fiftieth anniversary, it desperately needed a white knight, or at least some strong friends. It was about to get them.

•

Chapter 6

Building a New Central Library

Lon Tinkle, the respected book editor of *The Dallas Morning News*, wrote a column in February 1950 in which he quoted Nicholas Wredon, a vice president and editor at E. P. Dutton, calling the Dallas Pubic Library "shocking, absolutely shocking." The library, Wredon advised, needed a Friends organization, a group of citizens who could lobby on its behalf. Tinkle supported Wredon's advice; in fact, he wrote, he had been urging the formation of a Friends group for some time.[1]

Tinkle's column galvanized the library's leadership. Head Librarian Cleora Clanton, Assistant Librarian Violet Hayden, and library supporter Mrs. John Leddy Jones visited Tinkle to discuss starting a Friends group. As a result, on March 13, 1950, twenty-three citizens organized the Friends of the Dallas Public Library, electing Mrs. Jones president. Erin Bain Jones was a remarkable woman, a member of the first law school class at Southern Methodist University who went on to earn three additional advanced degrees at SMU. An attorney, author, philanthropist, and lay expert on environmental issues, she was a staunch supporter of education and served on the board of numerous civic organizations.[2] Leon Harris, merchant and author, was elected vice president and succeeded Mrs. Jones as president in 1951. Other early Friends included such distinguished citizens as Everette L. DeGolyer, geologist and book collector; Levi Olan, scholar and rabbi at Temple Emanu-El; Stanley Marcus, merchant and bibliophile; and Waldo Stewart, businessman and civic leader.

Library trustees Rabbi Levi Olan and Boude Storey accept the gift of a new bookmobile from Erin Bain Jones, president of the Friends of the Dallas Public Library, in October 1950.

The founders of the Friends had originally contemplated promoting the welfare of the library by sponsoring lecture series and acquiring rare book collections. But it quickly became apparent that the library had more basic needs. So the Friends adopted as their first project purchasing a second bookmobile to expand service to residential neighborhoods.[3] Within a few months they raised $6,000, and the new bookmobile was in service by October. The following July, Mrs. Elizabeth Ann Scott, who drove and managed the bookmobile, reported that she had checked out more than 71,000 books during the first nine months of service. Children's books represented the greatest demand. "Pajama-clad children, children on bicycles, mothers checking out books for their children crowd around the bookmobile at every stop." But adult use was also increasing.[4]

The fiftieth anniversary of the opening of the Carnegie Library almost went unmarked. With less than five days' notice, the Friends hastily planned a Golden Jubilee open house, complete with high school bands, punch, and a five-tiered birthday cake. The first guest to arrive was Folsom Fife, aged sixty-two, who had been one of the first three children to check books out of the library in 1901. Five hundred guests in all attended the event, including Mayor J. B. Adoue and several members of the City Council. Miss Clanton valiantly tried to shake every hand, and Mrs. Exall's son and daughter-in-law cut the cake. The Friends recruited forty new members. But the major news of the day was produced by a telegram from Bennett Cerf, head of Random House.

> Friends of the Dallas Public Library:
> All the way up here in New York it is a thrill to hear that at long last the citizens of Dallas are recognizing the deplorable disintegration of their public library and are now going out to bring it up to par with the rest of Dallas . . . It has always struck me as the height of the incongruous that a city boasting of some of the country's greatest bookshops and literary critics should also have one of the most run-down public libraries . . . Count me in if I can be of any assistance.[5]

Librarian Cleora Clanton and Dallas Mayor J. B. Adoue welcome guests at the Dallas Public Library's fiftieth anniversary celebration in October 1951.

This challenge from New York spurred the Friends to organize a campaign to build a new central library. The $1 million in bonds approved in 1945 were still unsold, but with inflation, it was now apparent that more money would be needed. With the support of the Friends, the library trustees asked the City Council for a place on the next bond proposal, and the council agreed. However, even before voters went to the polls, debate began over the best site for the new building. Former Mayor Woodall Rodgers was promoting a grand Civic Center immediately south of downtown. Could space for the library be created within the new City Hall? Or should it be a separate building? Should the old Carnegie Library be torn down and a new structure erected on the same site?[6] Property owners in the area targeted for the Civic Center, alarmed that their investments would decline, formed the South Side Association to fight the plan.

Concerned only to win support for a new library, the Friends tried to remain neutral. They decided to sponsor and finance a comprehensive library survey to study and make recommendations not only on the best building site but also on book collections, personnel, and management. To conduct this survey—the first ever undertaken in Dallas—the Friends retained two nationally recognized library authorities, Dr. Joseph L. Wheeler, former librarian of the Enoch Pratt Free Library of Baltimore, and John Hall Jacobs, head of the New Orleans Public Library.

On January 29, 1952, while Wheeler and Jacobs were beginning their study, voters went to the polls and—to the consternation of the City Council and the disappointment of the Friends—defeated the bond package. A month later the City Council abandoned the Civic Center project and released the southside property, except for land west of Akard Street designated for a municipal auditorium. The Council quickly assembled a second bond package that included $1.25 million for the library. Early estimates were that this money, combined with the $342,000 voted in 1927 and the $1 million approved in 1945, would allow for construction of a building with 125,000 square feet of floor space, compared with the 24,000 available in the old building.[7]

Representing the Friends of the Dallas Public Library, John William Rogers, Mrs. Lewis Lefkowitz, Leon Harris, Mrs. John P. Morgan, Violet Hayden, and Cleora Clanton present a petition to the Dallas City Council in December 1951 urging construction of a new main library building.

The Friends quickly went into action to win this second election. Their membership had by now grown to 1,000, largely through the efforts of Miss Edna Rowe, a retired

As part of a survey commissioned by the Friends of the Dallas Public Library, Joseph L. Wheeler conducts a street survey along Commerce Street in downtown Dallas in 1952.

school teacher who, in forty-seven years of teaching, had imbued three generations with a love of reading and a sense of civic responsibility. Stanley Marcus was one of several early Friends who had been students of Miss Rowe at Forest Avenue High School. As a result, the Friends now had a wide base throughout the community. They organized a public information drive, with a speakers' bureau, a series of television appearances, and campaign handouts. They set up a telephone bank and called all 65,000 library card holders in Dallas, urging them to support the bond issue on May 1.[8] As a result, the bond program passed by the largest vote in a bond referendum in Dallas history.

Wheeler and Jacobs had by now completed and submitted their report. Among their recommendations was that the new building should be "just as close as possible to the thickest pedestrian traffic." Their first choice was St. Paul between Main and Commerce streets. But if that location proved economically unfeasible, then the library should remain at its present site.[9] Following this advice, the library trustees voted a week after the successful bond referendum to raze the old Carnegie Library and build the new central library on the same site.[10] But former Mayor Rodgers, now a member of the library board, publicly criticized this decision, arguing that the site at the corner of Commerce and Harwood was too small, with no room for parking, and that it would be dwarfed by a twenty-story Statler Hilton Hotel, about to begin construction next door.[11] The Friends of the Dallas Public Library saw Rodgers' opposition as a veiled attempt to revive his Civic Center plan and expressed concern that the library could become a pawn in this divisive issue.[12] They were right. The debate over the best site on which to build the new library dragged out for nearly a year and a half. Not until October 1953 did the

City Council vote (for the third and final time) to build the new library at Commerce and Harwood.[13]

George Dahl, the most prominent architect in Dallas during the 1950s, was commissioned to design the new main library building.

The imminent demolition of the old Carnegie Library afforded the city an opportunity to restructure the governance of the library. Under the arrangement worked out in 1899, the management of the library was in the hands of a board of trustees nominated by the Dallas Public Library Association. This structure provided the library with a certain measure of independence from the city bureaucracy, but it also put the library at some disadvantage when it came to financial support. As the city auditor pointed out in a report in August 1952, the two-and-a-half-cent tax levy for library support had been insufficient for some time, and the library budget had been supplemented by "emergency" contributions from the city's general fund. The auditor recommended that, once the library moved out of the Carnegie building, the city should formally take the library into city government as a regular municipal department. The City Council would appoint members of the library board, just as it already did for other municipal boards. In their report, Wheeler and Jacobs had recommended just this procedure.[14] Roscoe L. Thomas, treasurer of the library board, supported the recommendations, saying that the trustees had been trying for some time to obtain more funds and tie the library more closely with the city.[15] The Dallas Public Library Association, whose sole function for the past fifty years had been to nominate trustees to the library board, thus came quietly to an end.

During the fall of 1952 the library commissioned architect George Dahl to begin drawing preliminary plans for a new building. Active in Dallas since 1926, Dahl's greatest achievement had been the Texas Centennial Exposition at Fair Park, twenty-six buildings erected in nine months in the depths of the Depression. He also designed a host of commercial buildings in Dallas, including *The Dallas Morning News* headquarters. He has been described as "a master of utilitarian architecture who was also capable of imaginative strokes."[16] Instead of a monument with a flight of steps and grandiose entry, like the old Carnegie building, Dahl's library would be sleek, contemporary, and with big windows at ground level so that passers-by could look inside.

Since the old building would have to be torn down before construction could begin on its replacement, the central library had to find temporary quarters. The Dallas Union Terminal Company agreed to lease the second floor of Union Station, comprising about 20,000 square feet, to the library for eighteen months at a cost of $28,000 a year.[17] "It was the only building in town that had the floor structure that would support our weight," recalled Lillian Bradshaw.[18] The old building officially closed on December 15, 1953, and 120,000 volumes were moved from the east end of downtown to the west. The library re-opened in its temporary home on January 2, 1954. The staff maintained a sense of humor about their new quarters. "The reference room is located right next to the tracks," one reporter noted, "making it one of the best sources of authentic railroad sounds possessed by any library anywhere."[19] Because the building wasn't air-conditioned, the doors opening onto the balcony overlooking Ferris Plaza had to be kept open during warm weather, inviting not only noise and dust but also pigeons.[20] But any discomforts could be en-

George Dahl had been the supervising architect for the Texas Centennial in 1936, transforming Dallas's Fair Park into an Art Moderne masterpiece. (Photo courtesy of the Dallas Historical Society)

dured, knowing that a modern library was finally at hand.

As soon as the library vacated the old building, workmen with Robert E. McKee Construction Company began demolition. Forty years later, protests would doubtless have been raised at the loss of this piece of Dallas history. But at the time, few regretted its demise. When the cornerstone was opened, it was discovered that moisture had destroyed most of the material placed inside in 1901, including maps, newspapers, and business cards. Only two business cards were still legible: one for "S. Heerdengsfelder, Dealer in Fine Cigars and Smokers' Articles" and another for a dentist, Dr. George Wilkins, "Don't have your teeth extracted; they can be preserved." Thirty-eight dollars and twenty cents in coins were also retrieved.[21]

Union Station, constructed in 1915-16 by nine railroad lines as the downtown Dallas passenger terminal, provided a temporary home for the Dallas Public Library in 1954-55.

The Friends of the Library hosted a reception on January 27 for the mayor and members of the Dallas City Council. Special guest was Bennett Cerf, whose telegram at the time of the library's fiftieth anniversary had helped rouse public support for a new building. Now, three years later, he told a reporter, "It is an advancement even to have the old building torn down. Now maybe Dallas will do something about a deplorable situation."[22]

That spring the Friends brought in another consultant, Francis R. St. John, chief librarian of the Brooklyn Public Library. St. John's task was to analyze the library's collections and identify its needs. "Your library here seems to be pretty weak in most fields for a city of this size," he observed, "but for the amount of support it has received in the past, it has done a better than average job of serving most of Dallas's needs." St. John said he was happy

Moving out of the old Carnegie Library after more than fifty years was a major job. Here Cleora Clanton confers with a mover.

to note that per capita expenditure for the Dallas library had risen from sixty cents to eighty cents in two years, although $1.50 was the accepted standard. He recommended the purchase of 650,000 books, at a cost of $1,375,000. The city should work out a five- to seven-year plan for gradual acquisition, and business and civic groups should be encouraged to develop collections in their fields. St. John also decried the rapid staff turnover. "Unless you can give better service when you move into your new library building," he warned, "you soon are going to lose the new loyalty and support the building will draw."[23]

One civic group had already pledged its support. Dallas Fashion Arts, Inc., a non-profit organization of women professionally engaged in fashion and related fields, announced its intention to establish a Fashion Research Center in the new library.[24] The apparel industry was a major factor in the Dallas economy, and its support for the library advanced its cause with other businesses. As the president of the Friends observed, it didn't hurt that "the aura of *fashion* miraculously descended upon the lackluster library."[25]

With construction underway and a new central library finally in sight, Cleora Clanton announced her retirement. For thirty-two years she had directed the Dallas Public Library, coping with inadequate budgets and deteriorating facilities. Lillian Bradshaw has described Miss Clanton as "indomitable" in her determination to provide the citizens of Dallas with the best library she could with the meager financial resources available. "She set her goals and never deviated from them, regardless of the chal-

During the twenty months the library was located at Union Station, staff and patrons had to contest with the noise of trains and invasions of pigeons, but it was the only available structure that would hold the weight of the book collection.

lenges."[26] She was also, in Mrs. Bradshaw's opinion, "a businesswoman before her time and a manager before her time," who dealt effectively with the city bureaucracy and her own often egotistical library trustees. She was a woman of high principles, who protested the exclusion of African-American librarians from the Baker Hotel during a Texas Library Association meeting in the 1930s.[27] And when a Dallas post of the Veterans of Foreign Wars protested the presence of three so-called "subversive" magazines in the library, Miss Clanton delivered an impassioned defense of intellectual freedom before the City Council. "We must not stop up the avenues of information," she said. "We must let the people find out what the enemy is thinking."[28] Early in 1952 Miss Clanton let it be known that she was contemplating retirement. She was sixty years old. "I've about reached the conclusion that a younger person should take over."[29] By the fall of 1954 she was ready to go. Her decision was apparently amenable to the library board. In a later interview, Lillian Bradshaw stated that she felt that the trustees decided they needed a younger person, preferably a man, to lead the library into the new building.[30] For public consumption, however, Miss Clanton was gracious, saying only that she had reached retirement age and was looking forward to doing lots of reading and some traveling.[31]

The old Carnegie Library was demolished in January 1954 to make room for the new Central Library.

In early November 1954 James D. Meeks, librarian of the St. Joseph, Missouri, Public Library, was named as the fourth director of the Dallas Public Library, effective the beginning of the new year. Meeks earned an A.B. from the University of Kansas City and a B.S. in Library Science from the University of Denver. He also had an M.S. in Library Science from Columbia. Prior to heading the St. Joseph library, he had worked in libraries in Denver, New York City, and Enid, Oklahoma. Meeks made a flying visit to Dallas in mid-November, meeting with Miss Clanton. Some librarians had expressed fears that the new home entertainment medium of television would hinder reading, but both Clanton and Meeks agreed that radio and television had actually stimulated use of books. Meeks had ambitious visions for the Dallas library. "We've got to be able to give service to everybody in town," he told a reporter. "To do this, I should think we'll need at least a book for every person in Dallas." (Since Dallas had a population of about 500,000, this was indeed ambitious.) "But they have to be the right books," he warned. "They must be useful ones that will meet the needs of the people here."[32]

At its first meeting in 1955, the City Council officially confirmed the selection of Meeks at a salary of $9,000, and it voted to retain Miss Clanton as associate librarian for six months at her present salary of $500 a month.[33] Miss Clanton was feted at a series of dinners and receptions, and then she quietly withdrew from the scene. As Siddie Joe Johnson, the long-time children's librarian who worked with Miss Clanton for fifteen years, wrote at the time of Miss Clanton's death in 1968, "Tenacity was the name for Cleora, this small, merry, bright-eyed woman." The new central library "was built with the mortar of her faith." "A book-lover who was not bookish . . . she was one of the greatest bookwomen Dallas has ever known."[34] The Friends of the Dallas Public Library decided to buy a rare book in her memory, and Mrs. Bradshaw

Library Board President Roscoe L. Thomas and Librarian Cleora Clanton opened the cornerstone of the Carnegie building on February 2, 1954, only to find most of the contents ruined by moisture.

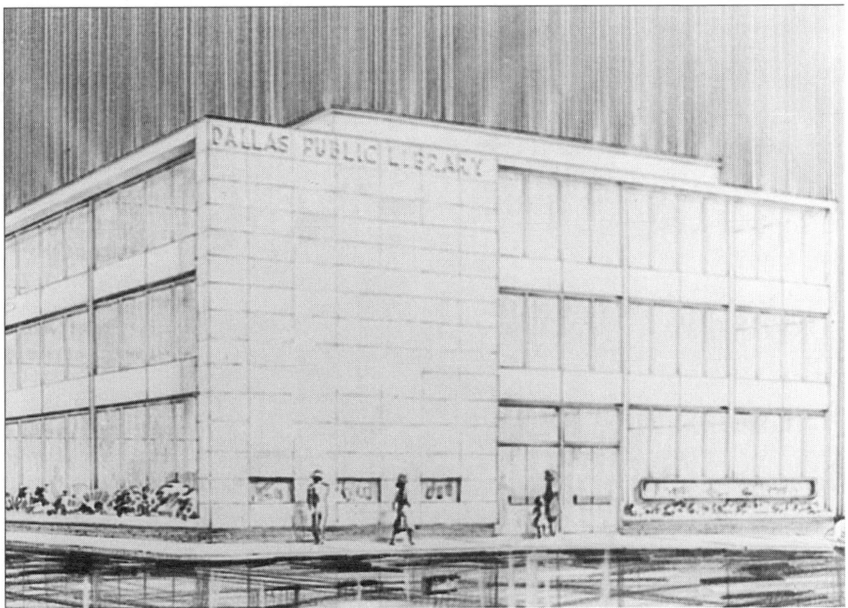

George Dahl's sleek, modernistic design for the new Central Library was a radical change from the classicism of the old Carnegie building.

and librarian Marvin Stone went to New York, "with a couple hundred dollars." After visiting various book dealers, they found an exquisite, medieval *Book of Hours*, which they carefully carried back with them on the airplane. This tribute remains, in Mrs. Bradshaw's opinion, one of the most beautiful items in the library's collection, a fitting tribute to a noble woman.[35]

Only thirty-four years old, James Meeks represented a new generation. "I'm not sure Jim ever read a book," Mrs. Bradshaw recalled, "but he was one of the best PR guys I have ever known. He was exactly what we needed at that time."[36] He was aware of the challenges he faced. "I've never doubted that libraries, especially public libraries, were the most important organization in a community," he wrote the Denver University Library School alumni newsletter shortly after taking the job in Dallas, "that good service was to be given at all costs, and that a librarian should never be through learning to be a better librarian, even if it means getting into jobs that are far over his head."[37] His first month on the job, Meeks presented a plan to reorganize the library into nine distinct departments, such as Young Adults (for which the Friends pledged $4,000), Local History and Genealogy, Fine Arts, and Children. Since these departments would require specialists (and since the new, larger library would require additional employees), Meeks asked for eighty-five new staff, which would effectively double the number working in the new building. The library board approved his request, but the City Council subsequently authorized only sixteen additional positions.[38] Excitement about the new library and its expanded programs began to generate gifts. With the announce-

James D. Meeks, thirty-four years old, was named as the new director of the Dallas Public Library in late 1954.

ment that the Fine Arts Department would lend phonograph records, the Junior League gave \$3,000 to purchase record albums.[39] And John William Rogers, the amusements critic for the *Dallas Times Herald*, presented 1,500 records including "collector's items" such as early piano and vocal recordings covering fifty years.[40]

As the new building neared completion in late June, the library was hit with an unexpected controversy. To adorn the main floor, architect George Dahl had commissioned a sculpture from artist Harry Bertoia of Barto, Pennsylvania. Bertoia had created a ten by twenty-four-foot metal screen consisting of a series of vertical bars from which varied metal shapes jutted out in three dimensions. The gilded shards of metal caught and reflected the light from different angles. The screen was hung over the circulation desk. Mayor R. L. Thornton called it "a piece of junk," although he added, "I'll say one thing—it'll attract attention. It has good advertising possibilities."[41] The newspapers had a field day. *Dallas Morning News* columnist Lynn Landrum suggested various names for the screen, such as "Big D Droodle," "This Frazzlin World," and "Carnegie Metal."[42] Aside from the inevitable jokes aroused by a piece of modern, non-representational art, some critics expressed outrage that the screen had cost \$8,500. "We think that to buy more books and things of that character for the benefit of the most people," said Mayor Thornton, "would be a much wiser investment for the taxpayers than a mural which only a limited number would understand and enjoy." In disgust, George Dahl paid for the screen and moved it to his home.[43]

Embarrassed by the controversy, which seemed to depict Dallas as a cultural backwater, several prominent citizens, led by Mr. and Mrs. Edward Marcus, Mrs. Alex Camp, Mrs. George W. Works, Jr., Waldo Stewart, and Patsy and Arch Swank, offered to

Following the public controversy over the cost of a metal screen designed by Harry Bertoia for the new library, workmen disassembled it and removed it to the home of architect George Dahl.

buy the screen and return it to its intended location in the library. The library board was amenable.[44] George Dahl agreed but exacted his revenge by insisting that the City Council indicate by letter its willingness to restore the screen. This the City Council did. *Dallas Morning News* columnist Paul Crume reported that a woman keeping a scrapbook counted 922 column inches about the screen, the equivalent of six full pages of newspaper copy.[45] The flap had certainly kept the library in the news, although it may not have been exactly the sort of attention the library might have desired.

By mid-August the library was beginning to organize its move into the new building. The carefully planned operation involved a small army of forty men and ten long trucks transporting some 250,000 books. Director Meeks was photographed riding down a conveyor belt from the second floor of Union Station with a book in hand. After decades in an inadequate facility, the Dallas Public Library was finally about to have a modern home.

•

After a group of private donors agreed to pay for the Bertoia screen, it was returned to its place above the circulation desk of the new library.

As if symbolizing the youthful image he intended to bring to the Dallas Public Library, director James Meeks poses for photographers riding down the conveyor belt designed to transfer books out of Union Terminal onto the trucks taking them to the new library. He is holding the last book to be taken from the temporary library.

Chapter 7

Settling In

The new Central Library opened for service on Tuesday, September 6, 1955. About twenty-five people were waiting outside when James Meeks opened the doors at 9 A.M. A city fireman, O. Z. Wallace, was the first person to check out a book.[1] Curious visitors explored the library's six levels (four above ground, two below), which included a roof garden, an auditorium, and exhibit rooms. George Dahl's open, accessible design provided 130,830 square feet of floor space and a book capacity of 800,000 volumes. Most of the shelving was freestanding, with few fixed walls, so that the size or location of a department could be fairly easily changed by moving bookshelves. The facility was completely air conditioned, insuring not only comfort for patrons and staff but proper climate control for the collections. Other modern amenities included three elevators, an automated book lift, and a drive-in book return at the rear. Among the inaugural guests were fashion designers Pierre Balmain, Vera Maxwell, and Florence Eiseman, in town for the Neiman Marcus Fashion Exposition Awards. They were duly photographed touring the library's new fashion wing.[2]

Some 3,000 people attended the formal dedication on September 25, at which Mayor R. L. Thornton snipped the ribbon. The mayor had by now changed his mind about the Bertoia screen. "I like it," he announced. "It was just when we thought it was a mural that we couldn't see anything in it."[3]

Without fanfare or publicity, the new library broke a major barrier. At a time when public facilities (including schools), hotels, restaurants, and most retail establishments in Dallas were still racially segregated, the Central Library was open to all. Library Director Meeks received a few letters from racial bigots, who objected to sharing the building with African Americans, but he ignored them.[4] An injustice dating to the founding of the Dallas Public Library at the turn of the century had finally been corrected.

The exterior of the new Central Library presented a somewhat blank appearance in June 1956, before the sculpture by Marshall Fredericks was installed.

The bigger problem for the library right now was all the empty shelves. For the first time in decades, the library had the room to accept donations. It immediately launched a book drive. In November, after the Dallas Alumnae Chapter of Sigma Alpha Iota, a national professional music fraternity for women, responded by donating sheet music to create a music lending library, the mayor proclaimed "Stock the Stacks with Music Week."[5] The next spring the City Council approved a special appropriation of $75,000 a year for four years to help build the library's collections.[6]

The Dallas Public Library had never collected fine and rare books. It had no budget for such items, and no proper place to store or exhibit them. But among the Friends of the DPL were scholars, writers, and artists who valued the book arts as a testament to literacy and civilization. The new library included a rare book room, which was named for Edna Rowe, the former public school teacher who had done so much to build membership in the Friends. The Friends set a goal of securing examples of book

Mayor R. L. Thornton presides at dedication ceremonies of the new Central Library on September 25, 1955.

arts from ancient beginnings to modern fine presses, along with exemplary types of paper, illustrations, typography, and binding.[7]

The new library also had space to present special exhibits. During the first year many of these featured items from private collectors, such as presidential autographs owned by Dallas attorney Dan Ferguson and a Gutenberg Bible loaned by the General Theological Seminary of New York.[8] The Dallas Society for Contemporary Art mounted an exhibit at the library, as did the Dallas Camera Club and other local groups. The new Central Library was quickly beginning to fill one of its goals, to draw the public back downtown for lively and informative cultural programs.

But the library couldn't seem to escape controversies involving art. In 1956 the Bertoia screen was joined by a second piece of art, a twenty-foot sculpture that hung against the black granite façade of the building. It depicted a young man, cradled in a giant pair of hands, holding up an open book. It represented the hands of God lifting youth in its quest for knowledge through literature, explained the sculptor, Marshall Fredericks.[9] Fredericks was a prominent sculptor whose works adorned the Detroit Civic Center, the University of Michigan, the Cleveland War Museum, and the U.S. Department of State building in Washington, D.C. In his preliminary sketches, the youth was unclothed, with nothing to limit his flight or discourage his reaching to the stars. "When we showed the board the model," recalled Lillian Bradshaw, "they almost died. It was a naked man. And what did they do? They voted to put pants on that sculpture."[10] Fredericks acquiesced, and when the 880-pound sculpture, cast in aluminum and magnesium alloy, was installed, the youth was modestly clad in trousers.[11]

Library Director James Meeks smiles for the camera on the fourth-floor balcony of the new Central Library, shortly before completion of the building.

A much more serious controversy erupted a few months later, when the library mounted an exhibit of paintings and hand-woven rugs by thirteen contemporary French artists. Among the works were a painting by Pablo Picasso of a woman's head and a rug designed by Picasso called "Keyhole." The exhibit opened on a Wednesday, and by Saturday James Meeks began hearing complaints that the library was displaying works by a supposed Communist sympathizer. He asked the advice of John Rosenfield, respected arts critic of *The Dallas Morning News*, who told him "to take the Picasso rug and picture down, that it was not worth the controversy."[12] Meeks followed Rosenfield's advice, arguing in a statement to the press that the library's main aim was "books, not paintings." "We think, perhaps, the library ought to save its strength to protect itself in case anyone attacks its books and tries to make us remove Communist-inspired books," the director explained.[13]

Empty shelves in the new library prompted book drives and donations.

The Dallas Museum of Fine Arts had only recently been bloodied in a similar battle, when ultra-conservative political groups had attacked it for patronizing artists whose political beliefs were "dedicated to destroying our way of life." The right-wingers had attempted to withdraw public funding for the art museum and urged trustees to purge the works of several "suspect" artists from a traveling exhibit on "Sport in America." The art museum board had waffled in its stance, incurring heated criticism from national art circles, but it finally stood firm against censorship.[14] With this example before him, Meeks felt it was important that the library pick its battles. "It is not that we surrender in principle. We just don't think it worth the effort to go through a siege of petitions, board meetings and period of tension at this stage of the library's organization and development."

Modestly clad in pants, a youth strives for knowledge in Marshall Fredericks' twenty-foot sculpture.

The library board backed Meeks, and despite some criticism from art circles, the library weathered this tempest.[15]

Meeks was perhaps more prescient than he realized when he cautioned that the library needed to save its resources to fight attacks on its fundamental mission—free access to books and periodicals of all political persuasions. As Dallas became increasingly conservative in the 1950s and early 1960s, such attacks were bound to recur. The VFW campaign that Cleora Clanton had fended off in 1953 would not be the last.

Meanwhile, the Central Library continued to expand its services. Just before the building opened, Meeks had stated his objective. "The concept of libraries has changed in the last twenty years," he said. "Libraries must stop being warehouses of culture and stress active means of attracting readers." A primary focus of the new building was its Young Adult Department, headed initially by Ray Fry, a specialist with three years of young adult work at the Enoch Pratt Free Library in Baltimore. Fry visited schools, churches, and clubs, giving book talks and reviews, and he presented a book fair to high school seniors demonstrating the richness and variety of the book world.[16] The Friends of the Dallas Public Library donated $3,000 to purchase 1,500 books for the division, and soon it began carrying films (mostly on sports and expeditions), hosting great books discussion series, and publishing a quarterly booklet, *Whangdoodle*, with books reviews and book news by teenagers.[17] In an era when the big department stores still had their flagships downtown, and Elm Street was still lined with

Teenagers produce an issue of Whangdoodle, *one of the innovative projects in the new Young Adult Department.*

first-run movie theaters, it was common for teenagers to ride the bus downtown and patronize the library after school and on weekends. The Young Adult Department filled an important need.

Ray Fry was typical of the young, professionally trained librarians whom Meeks was attracting to Dallas. Before Meeks's arrival, only a few staff members, such as Lillian Bradshaw and Margaret Pratt, head of the genealogy section, held library degrees. With the opening of the new library, Meeks got funds to add more staff, recruiting specialists to head the new divisions. He also encouraged young staff members, such as Tom Bogie, who had joined Dallas Public in 1950 after graduating from SMU, to pursue library degrees. In return, he promoted them to positions of responsibility, naming Bogie, for instance, head of the Community Living Department in 1956. Meeks was "just right" for the time, Bogie later recalled. He hired "very good, strong people," then gave them the freedom to develop their areas. He created a youthful, exciting atmosphere in which to work. "I always think of Meeks with a smile on his face," Bogie said.[18]

Adult services included chamber music series, book discussion groups, art and craft exhibits, and film series. Meeks was an avowed advocate of "merchandising the library," vigorously promoting its services to the public. In an article widely distributed by the Associated Press, Meeks described the new library's conveniences, including air conditioning, good lighting, and comfortable chairs. "The staff is good-looking," he observed, "well dressed and trained. . . . We're in the book merchandising business, and we've got to be modern to attract people."[19] Apparently his strategy was paying off. By

A Jaguar XK140 Roadster, parked in the Young Adult Department, was part of the library's celebration of the British Fortnight organized by Neiman-Marcus in 1958.

The Fine Arts Department developed rapidly in the new Central Library.

mid-August 1957, ten and a half months into its fiscal year, the library had checked out its one millionth volume (to Carol L. Neaves, a Lone Star Gas Company distribution engineer). This was a new record.[20] Another, more dubious, measure of success was the number of books stolen. In another AP story in December 1957, Meeks reported that the book most often stolen from the library was the Bible. Although he tried to keep about fifty copies of all versions in the collection, Meeks had recently had to order forty more.[21]

Meeks was quick to take advantage of opportunities to collaborate with other local institutions. When Neiman Marcus, Dallas's nationally renowned retailer, organized a French Fortnight in October 1957, the Dallas Public Library participated in a variety of ways. It published brochures on the French books, films, and music in its collections. It exhibited French documents and books from private collectors, as well as French posters. And it hosted an exhibit of historic French costumes from a Costume and Textile Museum in northern France. This first Fortnight was such a success that before it was over, people were asking Neiman Marcus, "What country are you going to feature next year?"[22] Thousands of people visited the store during the event, and since the fashion retailer was located only two blocks from the library, many also visited the library to see its displays. The next year, during the British Fortnight, the library showed daily English films and exhibited photographs, English antiques, and even an MG in the Young Adult Department.[23] And as the Fortnights continued for the next three decades, the library found itself with

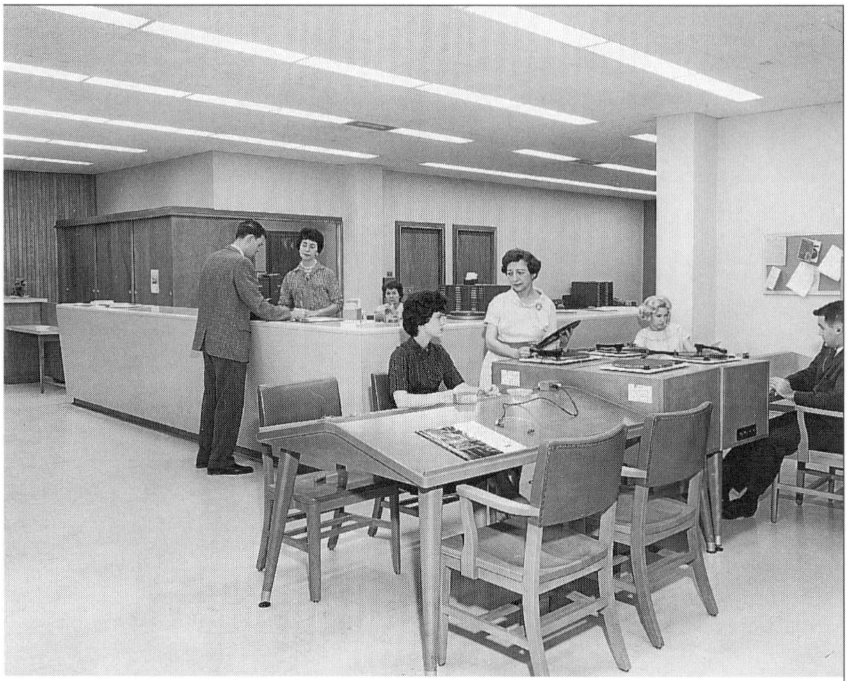

Masha Porte, holding record, assists patrons in the Audio/Visual Department in 1961.

an interesting subject and a guaranteed audience each October.

In February 1958 the library hosted its first Composers Conference. Funded partly with money donated by the Dallas Federation of Music Clubs, the Conference showcased the works of twenty-one contemporary composers. Solo and ensemble readings were performed in the auditorium at the Central Library, while the Dallas Symphony Orchestra presented orchestral performances of some of the works at the Music Hall. Among these was the premiere of Symphony No. 4 by Paul Creston, who served as moderator for the conference.[24] A second Conference in December 1960 featured the premiere of Darius Milhaud's Symphony No. 11 in C Major, specially commissioned for $1,500; Milhaud served as moderator for the Conference. The manuscript of the new symphony was placed in the library's special collections.[25] A third and final conference, renamed "A Festival of Contemporary Music," was held in January 1965. Jointly sponsored by the library's Fine Arts Department and the Dallas Symphony, this festival attracted 250 submissions. The commissioned work was the first symphony of Gunther Schiller, a composer, conductor, and critic of jazz as well as of classical music.[26]

These conferences did much to expand knowledge about and use of the library's growing Fine Arts Department, especially its music collection. In August 1958 one patron actually chose the department as the site for his arrest. Jerry Lee Cowart, age seventeen, of Jacksonville, Florida, went AWOL from the Army and attempted to rob a Dallas bank with a toy pistol. He then made an anonymous call to the police, telling them where to find him the next morning. And there he was, listening to a recording of Bach's French Suite #6 in E Major at the library. The ensuing publicity created a run on the audio-visual department; apparently many people hadn't realized the library had such resources.[27]

The library's collections in all fields continued to grow. The American Institute of Architects donated money for books on architecture. The B'nai B'rith Women of Dallas collected more than 5,000 books for the library through a two-week Book-a-Thon, for which Wyatt Food Stores permitted book deposit boxes in their stores and Sangers department store provided trucks. A local citizen died and left 1,000 books to the library. These were all donations in 1958. That same year the library acquired a new bookmobile, to replace the original one put in service ten years earlier. The new one was thirty-two feet long, weighed 22,000 lbs. (unloaded), and cost $23,000. It had a capacity of 4,500-5,000 books. The Dallas branch of the American Association of University Women raised money to buy books for the new bookmobile, which would service North Dallas (the Inwood, Preston Royal, Preston Center, and Walnut Hill shopping centers) and Pleasant Grove.[28]

Library Board President R. L. Thomas, center, welcomes new members John Read, left foreground, and Joy Schultz, right, in 1959. Standing are board members John Plath Green, S. J. Hay, Mrs. Edward W. Hard, Mrs. Dennis Colwell, and Leon A. Harris, Jr.

All these donations were an important sign of community support, but they were also essential because the library's budget, as always, remained inadequate. Director Meeks was especially concerned about staff salaries. In April 1957 he even declared that a "state of emergency" existed in the library because of inadequate salaries.[29] He was losing valuable employees to other institutions. Ray Fry, head of the Young Adult Department, left in 1958 to head the Rosenberg Library in Galveston. David Henington, who oversaw the literature and history department, was recruited the same year by the Waco Library to be its director. It

A Young People's Jazz Series attracted teenagers to the Central Library during the summer of 1961.

was a compliment, of course, that DPL librarians would be sought for directorships elsewhere. But Meeks found that he was often unable to fill vital positions because the salaries and fringe benefits were too low. He reported in April 1959 that the position of coordinator of adult services had been vacant since the previous May, and the assistant manager jobs in two other departments had been empty since October. He had had to prevail on the head of the catalog department to postpone her retirement because he couldn't find a qualified applicant. Now that the library was a city department, it had to compete with all the other departments for funding. And its employees were subject to the same salary and benefit caps as other municipal workers.[30] Meeks did gain valuable assistance when Lillian Bradshaw was appointed Associate Director on September 1, 1958, replacing Violet Hayden Dowell, who retired after thirty-five years with the library.

One of the local newspapers ran a long article about the library in October 1960, when the Central Library had been open just over five years. "Almost any afternoon will find a steady stream of youngsters in sneakers clutching science fiction books," the paper reported, "businessmen looking for facts that may mean money, and art lovers carrying prints or records pouring in and out of the Dallas Public Library on Commerce Street."[31] The following summer, the library organized a Young People's Jazz Series, with performances each Monday evening to standing-room-only audiences. In his report, Robert H. Dumas, Coordinator of Young Adult Services, asked, "Did the Project result in Progress for the library? In publicity, yes. In the humanizing of

Patrons of all ages use the Family Living Department in 1959.

the institution, yes. In stimulating circulation of books on jazz, yes. In inveigling non-library users into the library, yes."[32] Without question, the new Central Library, so long awaited, was a big success.

But Dallas was changing dramatically during the 1950s. With its geographic centrality, its modern airport, and a strong free enterprise climate, Dallas was among the fastest growing cities in the so-called "Sunbelt." From a population of less than 300,000 in 1940, it had exploded to nearly 435,000 by 1950, and to 680,000 in 1960. Its land mass nearly doubled after World War II to ninety square miles and continued to expand, as once-rural tracts became suburban residential developments. The completion of Central Expressway in the 1950s, along the route of what had once been the first railroad to reach Dallas, opened a major new artery for automobile traffic and encouraged development farther from downtown. Shopping centers followed, attracting consumers from the central business district.

To serve its customers, the Dallas Public Library would have to expand its system of branch libraries. With the new Central Library up and running, this would be its next challenge.

Telephone directories from across the country formed an important feature of the Reference Department in 1961.

By the 1960s, microfilm was becoming an important research tool, as this photo in the Science and Industry Department illustrates.

Chapter 8

Branching Out All Over

By 1955 the five branches of the Dallas Public Library were showing their ages. Oak Cliff was forty years old, and Dunbar and Sanger were over twenty. Oak Lawn was in a small, rented facility, and East Dallas was still in the one-time Cabell's building. All were overcrowded. The neighborhoods served by the branches had undergone significant changes. The old Jefferson Boulevard commercial district in Oak Cliff had deteriorated as new residential subdivisions with shopping centers were built farther south and west. The Jewish residents who had formed the core constituency for Sanger had mostly moved to North Dallas, and industry was developing in the area. The construction of Central Expressway only a few blocks from both Sanger and Dunbar had created a barrier through the middle of their neighborhoods and had left Sanger at the corner of a dead-end street.[1] Oak Lawn, the "Bohemia" of Dallas, was being rebuilt with apartments, while the independent municipalities of Highland Park (with its own public library) and University Park, which bordered Oak Lawn, separated it from the burgeoning neighborhoods of North Dallas.

The East Dallas branch, located farthest from the Central Library, was probably in the healthiest position. While the older neighborhoods south of it, such as Munger Place and Junius

Heights, were deteriorating, Lakewood and Lake Highlands were developing rapidly, bringing it a young and growing constituency. During the summer of 1955, its patrons helped raise money to air condition the building. "We had a little bucket at the desk where people could drop dimes and quarters and dollars," recalled librarian Marion Underwood. "We collected over $2,000." Builders Leo Corrigan and Edwin B. Jordan donated a used air conditioning system, and the library paid for its installation out of the funds collected. "We had about $500 left over," Mrs. Underwood said, "and we gave it to the children's library."[2]

In 1957 the Friends of the Dallas Public Library hired Dr. Lowell Martin of Rutgers University to conduct a study on branch library needs. Martin's report directed the library's expansion program for the next two decades. (Photo courtesy of Rutgers University Archives)

The following summer a developer planning a shopping center at Northwest Highway near Marsh Lane offered 5,000 feet at a modest rent for a branch library. The Bachman Civic League, representing residents in the north Dallas area, readily offered to head a campaign to raise $100,000 to outfit the facility and maintain it for a year. Soon a separate entity, the Northwest Dallas Branch Library Committee, was formed to oversee the project and, as its first effort, organized a book bazaar.[3] Such volunteer efforts, however, were no longer adequate to raise the large amounts of money required. Constructing branch libraries in the mid-twentieth century needed to be a coordinated, city-wide effort.

Having profited so greatly from the first two professional studies it commissioned—the 1952 Wheeler and Jacobs report on the Central Library and the 1954 St. John survey of the collections—the Friends decided to commission a study on branch library needs. To conduct the survey, they hired Dr. Lowell Martin, Dean of the Graduate School of Library Service at Rutgers.[4] Barely a week after his hiring was announced, the Southeast Dallas PTA began gathering signatures asking for a branch library in their area, which included the Pleasant Grove, Urbandale, Parkdale, and Piedmont neighborhoods, with a population of 150,000 residents. Canvassing the area over Memorial Day, the PTA collected 10,000 signatures and presented them to the library board, encouraging the board to work with landowners to see if they could get a site donated.[5] Clearly the desire for branch libraries was strong in all geographic areas of Dallas, and a professional survey was none too soon.

Martin conducted his study in early October 1957 and presented a ninety-page report in January. "Dallas has one-half a public library system," Martin wrote. The central building "is new, well located, and dynamic in its program." The five branches, however, "range from poor to fair in quality." Two-thirds of Dallas residents lacked adequate library service. Martin found this lack surprising, considering that Dallas had such an active business climate, healthy cultural organizations, and good schools—all of which depended on access to information available through a library. The central library alone was not sufficient. It was really designed to serve scholars, specialists, and those who lived or worked close to downtown. "The present surveyor," Martin wrote, "watched it in vain for a week looking for one of the most important user groups of the modern public library: the family group—father, mother and children together—each getting reading material suited to his needs." His conclusion was that families were out in their communities, "the natural location of family life."[6]

Use of the Dunbar Library had declined greatly by 1957, and Martin recommended closing it.

Martin recommended that, of the five current branches,

Vigorous support by the Friends of the Dallas Public Library helped pass a bond proposal in December 1958 that included $1 million for the libraries. Dallas Morning News *cartoonist Bill McClanahan captured the pride Dallas residents felt in the successful campaign, while a similar bond issue in neighboring Fort Worth had failed.*

Dunbar be closed, and Oak Cliff, Sanger, and Oak Lawn be relocated closer to the centers of their communities. Only East Dallas should stay where it was. Seven additional branch libraries should be built soon, most about six miles from downtown. Three more branch buildings would probably be necessary by 1970. Under this plan, each Dallas resident would have a branch library within ten to fifteen minutes driving time. Each branch should be located on or near important traffic intersections and in or adjacent to shopping centers. It should be clearly visible and have adequate parking space. Martin warned against the temptation to save money by placing a branch library in a park or on school grounds. Experience had shown that adults and family groups simply did not use libraries at such sites, which were often out of the way, dark and deserted at night. Libraries needed to be where people went, and shopping centers were ideal. Admittedly, such space was expensive. But "Dallas will simply have to face up to the fact that it neglected its branch library program for many years, when costs would have been much less, and now has no choice except to meet current price levels."[7]

Assistant Director Lillian Moore Bradshaw and Director James Meeks (both standing) and other library staff members review plans for new branch libraries in April 1961.

Martin's final recommendation regarding location was as follows: "Branch locations should be such that people of all racial and national backgrounds feel free to use the facilities; branch service in Dallas should be planned on a desegregated basis."[8] This was the major reason he recommended closing Dunbar. True, it had other problems. Its collection lacked "desirable scope and variety," and the facility offered no distinctive or special programs. The immediate neighborhood was deteriorating, with an increasing number of transients.

On August 3, 1961, Walnut Hill became the first branch library to open under the new expansion plan.

Declaration of Independence
Philadelphia: John Dunlap, 1776
Gift of Ira G. Corn, Jr., Mary C. and David M. Corwley, Dorothy and Robert B. Cullum, Sue and Joseph P. Driscoll, Margaret and Robert S. Folsom, Eileen and Joe Freed in memory of Eva and Dave Freed, Charlotte and Jospeh W. Geary, in memory of L. Storey Stemmons, Winkie and Jack Stroube, and Carolyn and A. Starke Taylor, Jr.

The name "United States of America" first appeared in print on this rare broadside printed on the night of July 4, 1776. This copy, one of twenty-six known to exist, is the only copy located west of the Mississippi River and one of the few copies on public display. A gift to the citizens of Dallas from a group of civic-minded citizens, the Declaration of Independence is housed at the Dallas Public Library in a special exhibit area provided by the Friends of the Dallas Public Library, Inc.

Mr. William Shakespeares Comedies, Histories & Tragedies
London: Isaac Jaggard and Ed. Blount, 1623
Gift of the Dallas Shakespeare Club in 1986 to commemorate the club's 100th anniversary

William Shakespeare died in 1616 without publishing any of the plays he wrote, and the few versions published by others contained many inaccuracies. Two of his friends, John Heminge and Hendry Condell, decided to edit and publish all of Shakespeare's 36 plays that they believed to be authentic. The work became known as the First Folio because it preserved, for the first time, the voice of the great playwright. The Dallas Public Library's copy, one of about 250 known to exist today, is permanently displayed in a special room provided by the Dallas Shakespeare Club.

Edward G. Eisenlohr,
American (1872–1961)
Fall in Oak Cliff
Oil on canvas, n.d.
Gift of the Quaero Club

Edward G. Eisenlohr moved to Oak Cliff with his family in 1874. Although he initially pursued a career as a banker, Eisenlohr studied painting with Frank Reaugh and other Texas artists and began to paint full time in 1907. This impressionistic view, typical of his landscape work, shows a scene along Cedar Creek. The Quaero Club, one of the women's literary societies involved in the initial movement to establish a library in Dallas, gave this painting to the Oak Cliff Library in 1922. Today, the painting hangs in the North Oak Cliff branch library.

Frank Reaugh,
American
(1860–1945)
Scene on the Brazos
Pastel on paper, 1883
Gift of the artist

Oak Cliff artist Frank Reaugh was a strong supporter of the effort to build a library for the citizens of Dallas. He gave this painting, one of his classic open-range landscape scenes, to the library for display in the art gallery of the Carnegie building. When the art collection was moved to Dallas' fledgling museum in 1909, Reaugh stipulated that this work remain at the library. It hangs today in the Special Collections division of the J. Erik Jonsson Central Library.

Babylonian clay tablet, ca. 2095 BC
Gift of the Friends of the Dallas Public Library, Inc.

This small lump of hardened clay is the Dallas Public Library's oldest work. The text is written in cuneiform, the letters pressed onto soft clay with a stylus before the clay was baked to harden it. These clay tablets were used to record information in a world where paper and the book were as yet unknown. This particular tablet is a receipt documenting the delivery of a shipment of reeds.

Herman Schedel
Liber Chronicarum
Nuremberg: Anton Koberger, 1493
Gift in memory of George I. Popper and George Arthur Popper

The most widely read and beloved piece of 15th century printing is this world history, commonly known as the *Nuremberg Chronicle*. It begins with the creation of the world and ends with the mid-1400s. Especially intriguing are the 1800 woodcut illustrations depicting the life and dress of the period, including this stunning two-page spread portraying the town of Nuremberg.

[Book of Hours]
Illuminated vellum manuscript. Northern France or Flanders, c. 1450
Gift of the Friends of the Dallas Public Library, Inc., in memory of Cleora Clanton

"Book of hours" is the name applied to prayer books used by the Catholic laity in the late Middle Ages. Wealthy people frequently owned sumptuous copies such as this one, which is distinguished by its intimate size, colorful miniatures, and beautifully decorated borders. The scene shown here is a fine miniature of the Virgin Mary's Assumption into heaven. This volume honors Cleora Clanton, the third library director, who served from 1922 to 1954.

Late Classic Serape Style Navajo Blanket, ca. 1875
Gift of Margaret and Eugene McDermott

The finely delineated design of this blanket is displayed against a brilliant red background. Serape style blankets are derived from Spanish and Mexican, rather than Pueblo, weaving traditions and are constructed of two vertical sections sewn together on one long edge.

Navajo Child's Blanket, ca. 1875
Gift of Margaret and Eugene McDermott

As synthetic dyes became available, the Navajo wove blankets like this one in riotous color combinations that dazzled the eyes, giving these pieces like this the name "eye-dazzlers." This smaller child's blanket is one of the McDermott collection pieces permanently displayed on the eighth floor of the J. Erik Jonsson Central Library.

Harry Bertoia, American (1915–1978)
Untitled [Textured Screen]
Steel, brass, copper, and nickel, 1954
Gift of a group of Dallas citizens

This monumental sculptured metal screen, which first hung over the circulation desk at the old central library building on Commerce Street, now gracefully spans the concourse on the first floor of the J. Erik Jonsson Central Library. Commissioned by architect George Dahl, the screen became the center of a major controversy when then Mayor R. L. Thornton, Sr., proclaimed it, "a bunch of junk" and indicated that City Council members felt that taxpayer dollars should not be spent on the abstract piece. A compromise was reached when a group of 71 donors bought the screen and donated it to the library. In the background of this view is Barbara Hepworth's 1963 bronze sculpture, *Square Forms with Circles*, donated to the library by Lillian B. Clark in memory of James H. Clark and Barbara Hepworth.

Photographs by Harrison Evans

Reginald Roberts, Director, Texas Region of the American Institute for Architects, presents an award to Dallas Mayor Earle Cabell and Library Director Lillian Bradshaw for the Walnut Hill Library, designed by architects Fisher & Jarvis.

Local residents would actually be better served by strengthening the Oak Lawn branch, which was only a mile away. But Martin's principal objection to Dunbar was that he could find no basis "for recommending separate service for a Negro neighborhood as such, whether one thinks of the rights of the people, the cost of facilities, or the legal obligations of a public agency." His recommendations were "based on an integrated program of library service."[9] While the Central Library had been racially integrated since its opening in 1955, Martin's observations indicated that custom, if not policy, was still keeping African Americans from using branches other than Dunbar.

The library board wasted no time in approving Martin's expansion plan, including his recommendation that future branch libraries not be built piecemeal, but as close together in time as possible, so that no sections of Dallas would be deprived. Martin estimated that this would cost about $2 million for the first phase, with $1 million more by 1970. The board distributed 1,000 copies of Martin's report to civic and community leaders. After the usual negotiations, the library arranged to be included in a $5.5 million Capital Improvement Program scheduled to go to the voters on December 2. The library's portion was only half the $2 million Martin had recommended, but it would provide a good start. It included $370,000 to buy sites for six branch libraries—in Walnut Hill, Preston Center, White Rock, Pleasant Grove, South Oak Cliff, and West Oak Cliff—as well as $630,000 for construction of two library buildings. The Friends of the Dallas Public Library and the library staff went into action, producing bookmarks, brochures, and posters showing the proposed locations of the new branches, and mailing out nearly 50,000 postcards to registered voters in the precincts nearby.[10] As a result of this vigorous campaign, Dallas voters approved the million-dollar program by the second highest margin of any item in the bond package.[11]

Participating in groundbreaking ceremonies for the Pleasant Grove branch library on October 6, 1960, were Library Board President R. L. Thomas, second from left; land donors Mr. and Mrs. Grady Wall, next to Thomas; and Library Director James Meeks, far right.

During the next year, the library began acquiring sites for the proposed branches and developing plans for the first two to be constructed. Given the strong community interest expressed by residents in the Walnut Hill neighborhood of northwest Dallas and the Pleasant Grove area in the southeast part of the city, it was appropriate that those areas would receive the first branch libraries.

A few adjacent homeowners objected to the proposed site for the Walnut Hill branch, at Marsh and Almazon, delaying acquisition somewhat. But the City Council finally approved it in August 1959, and the library board hired the architectural firm of Fisher & Jarvis to design the plans. Mayor R. L. Thornton turned the first shovel of dirt at groundbreaking ceremonies on September 23, 1960. Total cost for the facility was $343,327, including the land, construction, architects' fees, furniture, and books. Space was also provided to house the bookmobile. Mayor Earle Cabell, who had just taken office, presided at the dedication ceremonies on August 3, 1961. Walnut Hill thus became the first branch library completed under the $1 million expansion plan approved by voters.[12]

The Pleasant Grove Library opened to the public on November 10, 1961.

Mr. and Mrs. Grady W. Wall donated land on Buckner Boulevard for the Pleasant Grove branch, and George Dahl was retained to design the building. Unfortunately, when he presented his plan to the library board in December, the members rejected it as being too modernistic. They felt the straight roofline of the auditorium didn't harmonize with a series of gable-like effects created by a folded plate roof over the remainder of the building. One trustee said the building looked like a lean-to, while another said it would appear the trustees started out to be daring, then lost their nerve. Library Director James Meeks was diplomatic: "I have been more concerned in seeing that the interior was arranged for good service," he told a reporter. "It doesn't make any difference to me about the exterior."[13] Dahl presented a revised design to the board in April 1960, and ground was broken on September 30. The total cost for the building, including construction, architects' fees, furniture, and books, was $257,429.[14] Mayor Cabell presided at the dedication ceremonies and opening on November 10, 1961.[15]

The Pleasant Grove Library offered a spacious, modern facility for residents of southeast Dallas.

Both the Walnut Hill and Pleasant Grove libraries were attractive, even distinguished buildings, well designed for their locations. "We want each library to be as richly individual as its books and services," observed branch manager Wyman Jones. "It should be compelling enough to make everyone want to go inside. It must evoke a sense of personal welcome, because the bonds between books and people are personal."[16] Each branch opened with more than 30,000 books on the shelves, but with room to grow. Each

The Oak Lawn Branch Library moved into new rented quarters on Lemmon Avenue in 1960.

also had an auditorium, designed not only for library-sponsored programs but for community events.

During 1959 the library began acquiring several sites for future branches—Casa View, east of White Rock Lake on Ferguson Road; South Oak Cliff at South Lancaster and Corning; and West Oak Cliff at Illinois and Hampton. The site that proved most problematic was one for the Preston Royal neighborhood in North Dallas. Following Martin's advice to locate branches in high-traffic areas, the library board wanted a site on Preston Road just south of the Preston Royal shopping center. This site, however, would cost nearly $80,000. The city already owned property facing Royal Lane, 2,000 feet west of the shopping center and across the Cotton Belt railroad tracks, which it had acquired in 1956 for $8,500. To many observers, using this site seemed far more cost effective. The library board remained committed to Martin's advice, and the library consultant even wrote a letter arguing against the more remote site. As a result, the debate stretched out through 1960, evoking criticisms from the City Council and the North Dallas Chamber of Commerce. The library board recommended another site on Royal Lane—1,300 feet closer to the shopping center and on the same side of the railroad tracks—but it would cost $40,000. Finally, in February 1961, the board bowed to pressure and agreed to accept the city-owned site.[17]

Even in its new quarters, the Oak Lawn Library was cramped compared to the new branches being constructed around the city.

As for the existing branches, Oak Lawn moved into new, larger rented quarters at 3721 Lemmon Avenue, just south of a busy intersection, in March 1960. This branch had started life in 1929 as a deposit collection of children's books in the Sam Houston Elementary School, then moved in 1930 into rented quarters at 3014 Reagan, adding adult books. In 1950 it moved again, to larger quarters at 3521 Oak Lawn. However, by the time Martin conducted his survey in 1957, he found the library so crowded that if all three chairs at the single reading table were occupied, a user couldn't traverse the aisles.[18] The new quarters measured 3,200 square feet and contained 23,000 books, as well as new furniture and equipment. Unfortunately, the Oak Lawn library hadn't been open long when a Mrs. L. E. Allen complained of an "overbalance" of liberal books there. "We've got to have some books that explain communism, but we can't afford to have more than contrariwise," she announced. Roscoe Thomas, president of the library board, appointed a three-person committee to examine Mrs. Allen's complaints.[19] No action was taken.

The Dunbar branch was closed in 1959 and replaced by a small, rented facility in West Dallas.[20] The old Oak Cliff branch on Jefferson Boulevard was finally replaced in 1966 with a new building on the same site (see chapter 3). The Sanger branch, where circulation had slipped to fewer than 10,000 volumes a year in the late 1950s, doubled as headquarters for the bookmobile operation. In his study, Lowell Martin concluded that the building was now mostly a warehouse for the bookmobiles. Perhaps because of Sanger's utility in this regard, the library board didn't decide to close it until 1965. Then debate over the best location for a replacement branch to serve the residents of mostly black South Dallas delayed its actual closing until December 1967.[21] East Dallas (officially known as Lakewood

The Dallas Public Library opened a "storefront" branch in West Dallas in March 1959. It was replaced by a permanent building in 1975.

after April 1, 1958) remained in its old location until a new building was constructed nearby.[22] It took a dozen years after Martin issued his report, but with the opening of the new Lakewood library in 1970, all five of the "original" branches now enjoyed new quarters.

Lakewood residents gather for groundbreaking ceremonies for a new library building in their neighborhood in May 1969.

The success of the new branches was phenomenal. After only six months of operation, Walnut Hill zoomed to the top spot in the nation in branch library ratings with an average of 40,000 books a month being checked out. "Within nine days after opening the Walnut Hill Branch Library with 33,000 books, nine-tenths of all the volumes had been checked from the shelves," reported Wyman Jones. "We had to call a limit on the number of volumes that could be checked out and the number of weeks they could be kept."[23] Within a year, Walnut Hill had outstripped the Central Library in use. True, only 480,000 books had been checked out at the branch compared to 595,000 downtown, but the downtown figures included records, films, and pictures. Also, Walnut Hill was open only five days and two evenings a week, whereas the main building was open six days and evenings.[24] Pleasant Grove registered more than 300,000 books circulated during its first year of operation.[25] The citizens of Dallas were demonstrating, in unmistakable terms, their demand for branch libraries. Clearly, the immediate challenge for the Dallas Public Library was to continue the construction of new branches at a rapid pace.

•

Chapter 9

The Bradshaw Years

In mid August 1961 a small article appeared in the local newspapers, announcing that James Meeks would be leaving his position as Library Director at the end of the month. Meeks "had finished what he called his five-year program," announced board chair Sidney Latham, "and said he wanted to take what he called a sabbatical leave."[1] Under Meeks's leadership, the Dallas Public Library had opened the new central library building downtown and launched an ambitious program of branch development. Meeks had reorganized the staff and greatly expanded the services offered by the library. In a very real sense, he had propelled the library into the modern era. His tenure as director had been relatively brief, but it was significant.[2]

Lillian Bradshaw, the assistant director, was attending an American Library Association meeting in Cleveland, Ohio, when she got a telephone call saying, "You better come home. You're the acting director."[3] While most librarians had historically been women, the profession had changed considerably in recent decades, and by the 1960s, management positions tended to be held by men. A month after Mrs. Bradshaw took over, the *Dallas Times Herald* published an article pointing out that she was one of only three women in the country heading libraries in

Lillian Moore Bradshaw, who joined the staff of the Dallas Public Library in 1946, became acting director in September 1961 and was named director the following March.

large cities (the other two being in Chicago and San Diego).[4] Her credentials, of course, were impeccable, as was her reputation—she had just been chosen Librarian of the Year by the Texas Library Association. Nevertheless, the library board "spent a good deal of time trying to find a director that was a man," she recalled. "I was the only female to apply. Honestly, they tried very hard to find a male, but they didn't succeed. They could not get the vote of the board on any one male. So I was eventually appointed." She was officially named director March 1, 1962, at a salary of $11,000 a year—$1,500 less than had been paid Meeks. "Mrs. Bradshaw has national standing as a librarian and has demonstrated her ability here since she stepped in as acting director last year," announced board chairman Latham. "This is a highly proper and worthwhile step for the library to take."[5]

Given her years of promoting the library to the public, it's not surprising that one of Mrs. Bradshaw's first announced goals was to maintain the personal services of the library despite its growing size. "We want every subscriber to feel that we do our best to answer every question he has and to help him find the exact book or reference he needs," she told one reporter. The Dallas Public Library, she explained, currently had about 2,000,000 books and had issued 193,000 library cards.[6] To Mrs. Bradshaw, service "wasn't just sitting behind a desk and waiting for somebody to call. It was going out into the community. . . . You must learn your clientele. . . . You have to find out what their educational needs are, what their recreational needs are, what their hopes are. . . . In a way, the public library is an embodiment of every person that comes in the door, and you have the opportunity to work with that person just as that person needs you."[7]

In January 1962 Dallas voters overwhelmingly approved $1.5 million in bonds to construct four new branch libraries. The old bookmobile did its part to support the cause.

Because Mrs. Bradshaw believed that "a public library is just that—it is a library for the public . . . open to all," she firmly felt the Dallas Public Library "should collect things that interpret the past and the present." It had "a great responsibility to collect and store and save the materials of mankind."[8] Unfortunately, Mrs. Bradshaw's laudable goal of supporting open inquiry through books wasn't made easier by the increasingly conservative political rhetoric in Dallas. As one historian has observed, "In an era when fanatical right-wing extremism was gaining strength throughout the nation, few if any cities seemed more receptive than Dallas."[9] Reflecting this extremism was City Councilman Joe Moody, representing Pleasant Grove. Within days of Mrs. Bradshaw's appointment as permanent librarian, Moody charged that children could obtain "filthy books" from the Dallas Public Library. The two examples he cited were the novel *From the Terrace*, by John O'Hara, and a book of cartoons, *Hell of a Way to Run a Railroad*, by Peter Arno.

After she learned of Moody's charges, Mrs. Bradshaw went home and told her husband, "Honey, you may have seen the last of the current director, because I am going to fight this. I do not believe that an adult should be made to read on a child's level."[10] She issued to the press a vigorous defense of the library, saying it would be "reprehensible" to "denude" ("I loved using that word," she recalled three decades later) the collection until only children found it interesting. Children could not check out adult books, she explained, without written permission. "I believe adequate regulations

Library Board President Sidney Latham and Director Lillian Bradshaw were among the dignitaries who traveled to the sites of the four new branch libraries on April 24, 1963, for groundbreaking ceremonies.

exist to help a child select the literature best suited to his needs," she said. As for adult books, "you have to look at the purposes for which each book is purchased." Both O'Hara and Arno were social commentators, whose work often depicted valuable political, social, or economic history.[11]

Mrs. Bradshaw received widespread support from influential parts of the community. When one of her own board members, Mrs. David Schultz, called for a "head-count" of "liberal" and "conservative" books on the shelves of the library, Everette L. DeGolyer fired back with a letter stating that he was "simply appalled" at her request. "Instead of chasing the will o' the wisp of 'investigating' political balance—which certainly demonstrates a lack of trust in your employees by the very implication that an inquest is necessary—you might contemplate how to obtain funds to give Dallas the type of book collections it deserves."[12] The League of Women Voters chimed in with their support, commending the library staff "for its progress toward achieving standards of excellence."[13] WFAA-TV invited Mrs. Bradshaw and Councilman Moody to appear together to discuss the issue. Mrs. Bradshaw went, but Moody didn't show. "So what does the station do? They gave me the whole thirty minutes. I loved it!"[14]

Douglas Fain, president of the North Dallas Chamber of Commerce, turns the first spade of dirt at the groundbreaking for the Preston Royal Branch on April 24, 1963. Looking on are Library Director Lillian Bradshaw, Library Board President Sidney Latham, City Councilman Joe Golman, and children from Bette Hoffman Kindergarten.

At its next meeting, the City Council gave a vote of commendation to the library board, Mrs. Bradshaw, and the library staff. "In view of the splendid performance," of the library, the Council resolved, "it sees no need for evoking the doubtful policy and practice of attempting to censor library activities from the City Council table." Moody cast the only negative vote.[15] Mayor Earle Cabell, speaking at a Better Business Bureau membership campaign breakfast, sounded a strong warning against government censorship. "I am favorable to limitation of adult books to younger people, but God help us if we are jockeyed into a position where a government agency can tell people what they can read and what they cannot read."[16]

Leaders of East Dallas community groups participate in the groundbreaking for the Casa View Branch on April 24, 1963.

Fortunately, the library had developed a book selection policy a year earlier, as part of an overall self-study. The policy considered a number of factors, such as subject matter, permanent or timely value, and intent of the book, for the professional staff to follow in making their selections. Following the Moody controversy, the library board agreed to review the policy, but two months later decided not to tamper with it. The guidelines were appropriate and adequate.[17] Mrs. Bradshaw had undergone a baptism by fire, but she had emerged triumphant. The episode had established her as an intelligent, principled, and forceful director. As she later observed, the incident probably "solidified" her position in the city, alerting potential opponents that she would not be easily manipulated.[18] Without question, the Dallas Public Library was in capable hands.

Dallas voters had expressed their support for the library in no uncertain terms when they went to the polls in January and approved—by a four to one margin—$1.5 million in bond funds to construct four new branch libraries: in North Dallas (Preston Royal), Northeast Dallas (Casa View), South Oak Cliff, and West Oak Cliff.[19] The successful vote was to a large extent the result of a campaign spearheaded by the Friends of the Dallas Public Library that included 50,000 leaflets distributed in shopping centers adjacent to the proposed branch sites, 46,000 letters mailed to voters in crucial precincts, and thirty-second spot announcements on the radio. One of the bookmobiles sported a fifteen-foot banner reading, "Trade me in for a new branch library—vote Yes, January 23!" And despite a rare ice storm the day before the election, library supporters turned out to support the proposal.[20]

The library trustees decided to hire four different architectural firms to design the branches. Their hope was that each branch could have its own identity, reflective of its neighborhood, but that the architects would cooperate so as to achieve some harmony of design.[21] The plans were developed during 1962, and a multiple groundbreaking was held on April 24, 1963, with city officials, library trustees, and members of the City Council riding in a chartered bus from site to site with a police escort.[22] The festive occasion was sweetened by the news that the American Institute of Architects, the American Library Association, and the National Book Committee had just selected the Walnut Hill branch as the most outstanding library building constructed in the nation since 1958.[23]

Library trustee Clay Page, City Councilman Carie Welch, and Library Board President Sidney Latham break ground for the Lancaster-Kiest Library in Oak Cliff on April 24, 1963.

When the four new branch libraries opened in the spring of 1964, they again set records, especially in rapidly growing Northeast Dallas. As soon as Mayor J. Erik Jonsson formally opened the door of the Casa View library, children swarmed into the building so fast they tripped over one an-

Mrs. Frances Shoecraft, chair of the Hampton-Illinois groundbreaking ceremony, is joined by former City Councilman Dr. R. A. Self and Bill McCalib, manager of the Oak Cliff Chamber of Commerce, on April 24, 1963.

other. The crowd filled the entire library. Visiting librarians and staff members from the other branches and downtown pitched in to help. Hundreds of patrons waited more than an hour to check out books. Norman Graham, head of the branch, reported that 9,132 books were checked out on the first day. Subsequent correspondence with other libraries determined that this was the largest book circulation ever recorded for one day by an American library. During Casa View's first five days of operation, patrons checked out 25,000 books. About sixty percent of users were children, and Casa View was running out of juvenile fiction and nonfiction. Soon patrons were limited to checking out five books at a time and keeping them for only two weeks. The library board was also forced to extend Casa View's hours, keeping it open six days a week instead of five. "It's just an area that reads like crazy," said Wyman Jones, chief of branch services.[24] In July the board asked the City Council for an extra $45,000 so it could open a storefront branch in the Northlake Shopping Center, a few miles north of Casa View, to try to relieve the pressure. This branch opened in February 1965.[25] This storefront operation, and several that followed elsewhere in the city, helped "test" a neighborhood to determine demand for a permanent branch.[26]

The new branch libraries, of course, required professional staff, and Mrs. Bradshaw found herself fighting the same battle as her predecessors—hiring and retaining good librarians. A special committee of library trustees informed the City Council early in 1965 that the library was losing employees because of inequities in hiring

The Casa View Library was designed by the architectural firm of William H. Hidell.

and advancement as well as stiff competition from outside Dallas. The library was still operating under a salary scale drawn up in 1957, although its operations had expanded from six to thirteen units and its staff had tripled in size.[27] Good people were leaving the Dallas system, among them Lawrence DiPietro, head of the adult book collection since 1959, who accepted a position as head of the Topeka Public Library.[28] The City Council did agree to some select pay raises—including Mrs. Bradshaw to $14,000 a year—but this really didn't address the problem. As Mrs. Bradshaw explained to the library board, salaries in the Dallas system simply weren't competitive enough to lure qualified personnel.[29]

The library board approached City Manager Elgin Crull, asking him to hire a professional job analyst to study the library's job grading system. Currently the library had no way to reward an employee for carrying a heavier work load. Heads of branch libraries, for instance, were all paid the same salary, regardless of the size of the branch. Mrs. Bradshaw reported that she had been unable to fill several vacancies, notably the coordinator of children's services, the director of the South Oak Cliff branch, and the head of the science and industry department.[30] In October, a Philadelphia job analyst, Matthew Blitz, recommended that the city strengthen the system's base by upgrading entering positions. "This makes all the difference," Mrs. Bradshaw responded. "This is what we're after."[31] The upgrade may have helped some, but the library still lagged behind.

Yet the 1960s were exciting for the staff. David Henington, who had left in 1958 to head the Waco library, returned in 1962

Library trustee Mrs. I. V. Kipcak and Mayor J. Erik Jonsson (visible at the left) move aside as hundreds of children rush into the Casa View Library on opening day, February 29, 1964.

The Preston Royal Library, designed by William E. Benson, opened on March 21, 1964.

The South Oak Cliff Branch (Lancaster-Kiest), designed by Harper & Kemp, opened on February 8, 1964. The architects donated the horse sculpture in the porch area.

The Hampton-Illinois Branch, designed by Harold A. Berry, opened April 4, 1964.

as Assistant Librarian. The opportunity to work with Mrs. Bradshaw was an important attraction, but equally was the chance to be part of a dynamic team. Years later Henington recalled the stimulating discussions with his colleagues. "Everybody was excited about what we were doing," he said. "We were constantly doing something, growing. It was a very exciting environment in which to work." All the staff were young, "or at least *thought* young," he explained. Henington found his colleagues "really unusual in their professionalism and vision and what they were trying to do."[32] Many went on to head libraries in other cities, including Henington, who was lured to Houston in 1967.[33] But they got their start under Mrs. Bradshaw in Dallas.

As always, the Dallas Public Library persevered, despite inadequate budgets, creating new and exciting programs that drew the public. And again, as always, the Friends of the DPL lent its support. Following her censorship battle, Mrs. Bradshaw proposed a special exhibit "of great texts that I did not want anybody to take out of any library."[34] The Friends underwrote the costs of the exhibition, entitled "Words That Changed the World," which opened in November 1963. Chaired by J. Erik Jonsson, a longtime Friend and later mayor of Dallas, the show was designed by architects, with a catalogue written by Decherd Turner of SMU's Bridwell Library. The sixty-four items in the exhibit, dating from 1554 to 1943, displayed works that shaped human destiny, written by such figures as Aristotle, Martin Luther, John Milton, and Charles Darwin. Many of the items belonged to local private

Library trustees open a storefront branch in the Northlake Shopping Center on February 13, 1965, to relieve pressure on Casa View.

The Friends of the Dallas Public Library underwrote a special exhibition, "Words That Changed the World," that opened in November 1963.

collectors, such as Sawnie Aldredge, Everette L. DeGolyer, and Albert Outler. The Lilly Library at the University of Indiana loaned a First Folio of Shakespeare and Thomas Jefferson's personal copy of the first printing of the Bill of Rights.[35] This exhibit was followed in 1965 by "The Legendary West," examining fact and fiction in the history of the American West. In 1967 Friends Eugene and Margaret McDermott underwrote "The Arts of the French Book, 1900-1965," with an award-winning catalogue published by the SMU Press. And in 1970 the Friends mounted "Heritage of Freedom," showcasing thirteen rare icons such as the Mayflower Compact, loaned by the Newberry Library in Chicago; a copy of the Declaration of Independence, owned by two Dallas collectors; the Constitution from the Library of Congress; the Bill of Rights from the Lilly Library; and the Emancipation Proclamation from Brown University Library.[36]

While these exhibits featured rare books and printed material loaned by generous individuals and institutions, the Friends of the DPL also began acquiring treasures for the library's own collection. During the 1960s and 1970s, Friends arranged to purchase or donate illuminated manuscripts; examples of early printing by Gutenberg, Jenson, Caxton, and Aldus Manutius; examples of fine printing by Ashendene, Kelmscott, and Doves; the *Nuremberg Chronicle* and the *Oxford Lectern Bible*; and many other rarities.[37]

In time, the library would mount significant exhibitions consisting entirely of works it was preserving in its own collection.

"Mr. Peppermint" (portrayed by Jerry Haynes), host of a popular children's program on WFAA-TV, promotes use of the library with librarian Beverly Dotson in August 1963.

The acquisition and exhibition of rare books, of course, represented only a small portion of the library's regular program. Story hours, puppet shows, and summer reading programs at all the branch libraries reached thousands of children. The library worked with the Police Department's Youth Services Division to offer tutorials in reading for juvenile first offenders. The library also cooperated with the school district in assisting adults to acquire high school equivalency diplomas. Until all the branches were built, a new bookmobile was put in service, capable of holding 4,500-5,000 books.[38] By the mid-1960s, the library was answering more than a million reference questions each year, compared to a quarter of that number ten years earlier. Nearly three and a half million books circulated in 1965.[39]

Lillian Bradshaw's service-oriented policies were clearly paying off. The Dallas Public Library was becoming an integral part of the lives of hundreds of thousands of Dallas residents, and one of the city's proudest assets. But success also brought problems—more and more new books, periodicals, and other materials to be acquired, at ever escalating costs; older books to be rebound or replaced; not enough staff to meet all the needs. Some far-sighted individuals were even recognizing that the Central Library—only ten years old—would need to be replaced with a larger facility before long. The man who, more than any other, helped to realize this last dream was the new mayor of Dallas, J. Erik Jonsson.

•

Chapter 10

Setting and Fulfilling Goals

J. Erik Jonsson was a wealthy, self-made industrialist who had played a key role in transforming Texas Instruments into a worldwide firm on the cutting edge of technology. Jonsson was known as a visionary, good at planning and goal setting. When Earle Cabell resigned as mayor of Dallas to run for Congress in 1964, the City Council asked Jonsson to fill the position. Dallas had been the scene of a national tragedy a year earlier, when President John F. Kennedy had been assassinated while riding in a motorcade through downtown. It had been labeled a "city of hate," and its residents often found themselves the target of insults when they traveled elsewhere. Dallas desperately needed a leader to help it recover its spirit. Erik Jonsson proved the perfect man for the job.

One of Jonsson's most imaginative projects was "Goals for Dallas," a city planning effort, but one with a difference. Instead of being confined to "bricks and mortar" issues like traffic patterns and water supplies, Goals for Dallas was much broader in scope. Jonsson asked citizens to help come up with common goals for such areas as local government, health and welfare, education, cultural activities, and recreation. He wanted to involve as many people as possible—not just city planning experts or civic leaders—and he wanted them to dream, to envision the very best for Dallas.[1]

J. Erik Jonsson, who served as Mayor of Dallas from 1964 to 1971, was one of the Dallas Public Library's strongest supporters.

When the initial idea for Goals for Dallas was announced in November 1964, the library wasn't included. "Well, I couldn't stand that," recalls Mrs. Bradshaw, "so I wrote to Mr. Jonsson and said, 'Hey, you cannot talk about the future of Dallas without talking about education, and when you talk about education then you have to include the public library.' Well, Erik Jonsson was a man of very broad vision, and he was also a gentleman that really never turned down any opportunity to get more information. So I was invited to join the [planning] group." Out of a retreat in Salado, Texas, in June 1966, attended by eighty-seven men and women with a wide range of racial, professional, and economic backgrounds, came endorsement not only of additional branch libraries, but of a new Central Library as well.[2]

Following a series of public meetings throughout the city, at which a host of ideas was discussed, reviewed, and refined, the Goals for Dallas office published reports describing proposed projects. In April 1967 Mayor Jonsson and a team of architects and city planners made the first official presentation of proposals for a new City Hall and a group of other civic facilities, including a Central Library. Among the presenters was architect I. M. Pei (who would eventually design the City Hall).[3] Ironically, the proposed site for this complex of civic structures was along Young Street, on the southern edge of downtown, exactly where Mayor Woodall Rodgers had wanted it nearly two decades earlier. Dallas had changed greatly in fifteen years. Joseph Wheeler and John Hall Jacobs had written in their 1952 survey that "parking is not the library's problem," since ninety-five percent of its use came from men and women downtown to work or shop.[4] As a result, the building constructed in 1955 offered no parking, only a loading dock at the rear. But people who didn't work downtown increasingly did their shopping in neighborhood centers, and with restaurants, stores, and movie theaters abandoning downtown, pedestrian traffic was declining steadily. The streetcar tracks were removed from downtown, leaving buses as the only form of mass transit. Mayor Rodgers had been right: the library did need to offer parking if it was to attract Dallas's automobile-dependent citizens, and so did City Hall and other civic buildings.

The first bond election to result from Goals for Dallas was called the "Crossroads" program, signifying that the city had an opportunity to step boldly into the future. The Crossroads program included $2.325 million for libraries (out of a $175 million total package). The money would fund construction of four new branches and purchase sites for three more. The Lakewood library would be replaced with a new building nearby, and a new Northlake facility would replace the leased one. Two new branches would be built in Northwest Dallas and in Southwest Oak Cliff. Sites would be acquired near Hillcrest and Arapaho in far North Dallas, at Forest Lane and Greenville, and in Southeast Dallas (the Skyline Branch, which opened in 1977 on Everglade). The bond issue also included $41.2 million for a new city hall with adjoining park-plaza and underground parking garage. More than 80,000 voters went to the polls in August 1967—a record turnout—and all fourteen propositions passed.[5]

A storefront library opened on Forest Avenue January 8, 1968, to replace the old Sanger Branch.

That December the old Sanger branch library finally closed, and a new, temporary facility was opened on Forest Avenue to replace it. The new South Dallas branch held 16,000 books and was operated by a staff of five. At the

A branch library and learning center became part of the new Martin Luther King Community Center on Forest Avenue.

dedication, South Dallas Chamber of Commerce President Joe Kirven told the audience that he hoped the new branch would be "used so extensively that in the next few years we may have to build a larger and better facility."[6] In fact, later that year the City Council approved architectural plans for a South Dallas community center (eventually named in honor of Dr. Martin Luther King) that would include a 10,000-square-foot library as one of several buildings in the complex.[7]

With the replacement of the original Oak Cliff branch library in 1966 (see Chapter 3), this left only Lakewood—of the early branches—in its original building. Mayor Jonsson, Mrs. Bradshaw, and Woodrow Wilson High School student Carl Shepherd (representing young adult readers) participated in groundbreaking ceremonies in May 1969 for a new library building a block away from the old site. The new Lakewood library opened a year later.[8] The city sold the old Cabell's ice cream parlor building for $56,130 and applied that money toward the $256,000 cost of the new library. One of the city's first historic preservation controversies arose in 1974, when it was learned that Pizza Hut had a contract to buy the old building, with plans to construct a restaurant on the site. The City Plan Commissioner's Historic Preservation Committee designated the old library building as one of the ten most historic structures in Dallas (along with Sacred Heart Cathedral, the Belo Mansion, and the Wilson and Kirby buildings), and citizens concerned at the possible loss of the former library building besieged city hall with petitions. As a result, the Board of Adjustment granted a parking variance that would allow the building to be remodeled for

The new Lakewood Branch Library opened in 1969 only a block from the site the branch had occupied for thirty years.

commercial uses. Pizza Hut let its option die, and a new group called the East Dallas Development Corporation, organized by twenty businessmen and residents in the Lakewood area, acquired the building. They signed leases with Exchange Savings & Loan and with the City of Dallas, which planned to place some offices of its Housing Department there. Thus the picturesque, white stone building, rich in memories for Lakewood library users, was preserved.[9] Since Oak Cliff, Dunbar, Sanger, and the early sites of the Oak Lawn library have all been demolished, the East Dallas building is the earliest branch library building still standing in Dallas.

Meanwhile, construction of more new branches was continuing apace. Mayor Jonsson and Mrs. Bradshaw broke ground in November 1969 for the Audelia Road library in Northeast Dallas. Built at a cost of $675,000, it had a capacity of 69,000 books in 13,089 square feet of space. When it opened in March 1971, it replaced the rented storefront operation in the Northlake Shopping Center.[10] In December 1969 the mayor and library director went to the opposite side of town to break ground for the Polk-Wisdom branch. This facility would cost $715,000, include 15,700 square feet, and have shelf space for 63,000 volumes.[11] In February 1970 Mayor Jonsson and Mrs. Bradshaw were in Northwest Dallas, on Forest Lane at Cromwell, to break ground for the Park Forest branch library.[12] Plans were on the drawing board for new branch libraries in far North Dallas at Hillcrest and Belt Line (Fretz Park) and in Northeast Dallas on Forest Lane near Greenville.

The Audelia Road Branch Library opened in March 1971, replacing the storefront operation at the Northlake Shopping Center.

Ironically, the fact that Dallas had launched its massive

branch library building campaign rather late proved to be a benefit, at least in some regards. "We learned from the mistakes of others who had put branches in parks and quiet places," Mrs. Bradshaw explained in 1968. "Their libraries were not used." Dallas, on the other hand, was "one of the few metropolitan library systems in the country where library usage is climbing." "Libraries must follow good merchandising practices, and this includes the locations with people. We try to locate branches where people come to shop and conduct a daily round of activities, places convenient to all the family at one fell swoop." At a busy center, the library director pointed out, operational costs (per patron) were actually less, while the educational value was greater.[13] In general, the location for each branch was selected to serve residents within a two-mile radius. It needed to be accessible by public transportation, but the site also needed enough space for parking.[14]

The Dallas Public Library also tried to tailor each branch to serve its particular neighborhood. Mrs. Bradshaw told the City Council in 1969 that she saw the public library as a "people-oriented educational service for each and every citizen—the businessman, housewife, scientist, student, minister, mechanic." Its responsibility spread from the preschooler to the senior citizen, and from the functionally illiterate to the technical researcher. The library's challenge was to meet the needs of different neighborhoods, "from the affluent areas of North Dallas to the poverty pockets of West Dallas," while serving such a diverse constituency. One solution was the daily shuttle service among all the branches and the Central

The Polk Wisdom Branch Library opened in 1970.

Library, which could provide twenty-four-hour delivery of any book requested. Mrs. Bradshaw's principal frustration was that the library's budget wasn't adequate to keep the branches open more than five days a week.[15]

The Park Forest Branch Library opened in 1971, serving residents of far Northwest Dallas.

By 1971 the city had successfully acquired most of the land targeted for Mayor Jonsson's new civic center complex. The library's architectural consultant recommended construction of a new $14.1 million Central Library in the area. Donald Jarvis of Jarvis Putty Jarvis, Inc. (who had designed the award-winning Walnut Hill branch library) felt there was no point in trying to expand the current 125,000-square-foot library. Instead, the city needed to build a new, 300,000-square-foot facility that could later be expanded to 600,000 square feet. Although the cost seemed dauntingly high, the library staff began studying Jarvis's recommendations.[16] Another bond election in June 1972 provided $5 million for library facilities, including design and construction of three new branch libraries and site acquisition for three more branches. It also included $315,000 in design fees for a new Central Library.[17] The project was, slowly but surely, inching forward. That fall the City Council approved use of a tract bounded by Young, Browder, Wood, and Ervay streets as a site for the new Central Library. A performing arts center, originally envisioned for that land, could go elsewhere.[18] With the land identified, Mrs. Bradshaw asked the City Council to include $18 million in funding in the next bond election.[19]

Meanwhile, the current Central Library was getting overcrowded. Hallways were being used for storage. The aisles be-

In 1972 the library leased space in the Wholesale Merchants Building (left) at 912 Commerce to relieve overcrowding at the Central Library.

tween the stacks were only twenty-seven inches wide (whereas library standards called for thirty-six inches), meaning the staff couldn't push a cart of books down the aisle to reshelve them. Research space was limited, and microfilm viewers shared brightly lit space with others, rather than being in a darkened area. Mrs. Bradshaw brought the problem home to the library trustees in September 1968 by informing them that they would have to find another location for their meetings, as the space occupied by the Board Room was needed for offices; the next month they started meeting in the Rare Book Room.[20] In July 1972 the city agreed to a seven-year lease at $8,000 a month for the Wholesale Merchants Building at 912 Commerce. With 31,000 square feet of floor space, this facility could serve as an annex for storage of infrequently used library materials and as work space for technical staff services. When briefed on this lease, Councilman George Allen objected, arguing that the city could purchase a building for $400,000, spend $1 million fixing it up, and thereby own and use it for many more years than the leased facility. After thinking about it for a week, the rest of the City Council decided Allen had a good point, and they tried to renege on the deal. But they were too late. The lease had already been executed.[21] The film library was moved to the annex, along with ten operational units such as materials processing staff (cataloguing, binding, etc.) But the two-building arrangement was inconvenient.[22]

A new Central Library could come none too soon. In June 1973 the city hired Fisher and Spillman Architects, Inc., to design the new building. The firm had won an award in 1971 for its

The Fretz Park Branch Library opened in 1976, following a vigorous campaign by area residents.

The Dallas West Branch Library opened in 1975.

design of the new Lakewood library.[23] The library staff asked Fisher and Spillman for a building of "architectural distinction and beauty," whose design would also "reflect the Library as a people-place, accommodating a variety of users involved in a multitude of ever-changing activities in an atmosphere of confidence and trust." The new building also needed to encompass "the most advanced applications of technology and communications systems, including the computer."[24]

While planning for a new Central Library proceeded, the system continued to add more branches. Ground was broken in June 1974 for new branches in West Dallas and Fretz Park. The Dallas West library on Singleton Boulevard replaced a rented storefront operation. Constructed at a cost of $1.5 million, it opened in August 1975 with 50,000 books in 15,000 square feet of space.[25] The opening of the Fretz Park library on Belt Line Road in January 1976 marked the culmination of more than six years of effort by its North Dallas community, led by the Northwood Women's Club. Area residents campaigned to pass the 1972 bond issue that funded construction, a local garden club helped landscape the facility, and an Eagle Scout group counted the more than 68,000 volumes that went on the shelves.[26] Yet another bond election in December 1975 provided funds for new branches in Oak Lawn and Highland Hills.

The Dallas Public Library was also able to use some federal Community Development grants to update the older branches with new carpeting and paint. And it created three community outreach positions to assist the branches in presenting programs to PTAs, senior citi-

A 1975 bond election provided funds to build a new branch library for Oak Lawn, the first permanent structure for the community after forty-five years in rented facilities.

Highland Hills Branch Library, in far South Dallas, opened in 1980.

zens, schools, and other neighborhood groups. To afford greater efficiency in purchasing, the library designated certain branches as repositories for books in certain fields—art, for instance—depending on the perceived interests of the community. The continued development of the inter-library loan system among the branches and the Central Library meant that it was no longer necessary for each branch to duplicate the holdings of the others.[27]

As new branch libraries opened on the outskirts of Dallas, closer to suburban communities, the old debate resumed on whether to charge nonresidents for borrowing privileges. In 1975 the library's circulation director, Allie Flo Voss, estimated that nonresident borrowers numbered about 76,000 out of the 486,000 who used the facilities, or about sixteen percent. Each book checked out of the library represented an expense (in staff time to process the transaction, reshelve the book, follow up with overdue notices when necessary, as well as wear and tear on the book, etc.), yet nonresidents contributed nothing through taxes to support the library. Dallas taxpayers paid, on average, eight dollars a year to support the library system. In December 1975 the City Council voted to establish nonresident user fees effective January 1, 1976. Library cards would cost $8.50 for 50 books, $12 for 100 books, and $35 for 400 books.[28] Librarians in Farmers Branch, Carrollton, Grand Prairie, Garland, and other suburban communities all reported a marked increase in circulation following the implementation of the fee. Yet during the first two months the policy was in effect, the Dallas Public Library sold 1,727 fee cards, bringing in $17,882 in revenue. Assuming that each card repre-

The Skyline Branch Library opened in 1977.

Groundbreaking for the Forest Green Branch Library took place on November 23, 1974, and the building opened to the public February 28, 1976.

sented a family of three or four, this meant that several thousand nonresidents considered the Dallas Public Library a benefit worth paying for.[29]

With much more to celebrate than it had had twenty-five years earlier, the Dallas Public Library planned a number of activities to mark its seventy-fifth anniversary in the fall of 1976. Lillian Bradshaw and Mayor Robert Folsom cut a giant cake to inaugurate the festivities. Among the guests was Mrs. Henry Exall, Jr., who had participated in the fiftieth anniversary reception and whose mother-in-law had led the drive that created the library. Stanley Marcus, one of the founding Friends of the library, chaired a symposium called "The Arts—Who Pays?" exploring the interrelationship of the arts, business, and government. Marcus and his wife also loaned their collection of miniature books for a special exhibition at the downtown library, complete with a miniature book specially published for the occasion, entitled *Why Miniature Books?* Each branch library (of which there were now sixteen) also mounted a special exhibition and hosted celebratory events. (Walnut Hill, for example, held a chili cookoff, judged by noted authorities Frank X. Tolbert and Billy Porterfield, with the winner receiving a lei of chili peppers.[30]) A Librarians' Dinner program featured a panel discussing the topic, "Urban Libraries and Librarians: Future Prospects." Most of the panelists were former Dallas Public Library employees who had gone on to head major libraries around the country. Free noontime programs at the downtown library featured performances by Dallas ballet, theater, and opera groups. And the library commissioned journalist Larry Grove to write a history of the institution's first seventy-five years.[31]

Grove devoted a twenty-page chapter to "Today," examining the strengths of the library's many divisions, from Fine Arts to Genealogy, from Children's and Young Adult Services to Business and Technology. In 1976 the Dallas Public Library's holdings numbered 2,396,000 items, including books, films, cassettes, and magazine titles. Circulation during 1974-75 had been over 4 million. But as Grove pointed out, numbers were only a small part of the story. The library's success was due to the fact that the staff had carefully studied the needs of its constituency and had formulated goals in five areas: user-oriented service, materials collection and selection, organization of materials, staffing and management, and communications. These goals were explored in a booklet published in 1972 that was praised by *Library Journal* as "a fine set of library aspirations, plus a large number of nuggets of innovation and new thinking."[32]

Grove's final chapter was entitled, "Tomorrow." It offered some tantalizing glimpses of the proposed new Central Library. This goal, sought for more than a decade, was finally heading toward realization.

•

After seventy-five years of providing free services to nonresidents, the Dallas Public Library began charging fees in January 1976.

Each branch library got its own cake during the library's seventy-fifth anniversary celebration.

Chapter 11

Riding the Wave of Success

While the 75th anniversary celebration was underway, the Dallas City Council unanimously approved design plans for a new Central Research Library and authorized Fisher and Spillman Architects to proceed with working drawings. The architects had proposed a ten-story structure including two basement levels, the lower of which would be reserved for a public parking garage. At street level, a pedestrian mall would cut diagonally across the building from the corner of Ervay and Wood to a plaza facing I. M. Pei's City Hall. A total of 2.3 million volumes could be stored on the seven floors given over to subject areas; total square footage was more than 600,000. Working with library staff, the architects came up with the idea of giving each department part of its floor as a closed area, both for staff office areas and for storage of rare materials or items kept on reserve. This way, staff wouldn't need to be running up and down in the elevators to retrieve materials. Fewer staff could function more efficiently.[1]

Construction costs were estimated at $37 million, with the total price (including furniture, equipment, and professional fees), reaching $44 million. The City Council also directed the city manager to study funding possibilities, including application for $4.5 million in federal Public Works Employment funds.

This architect's rendering of the new Central Library shows the north façade, facing Wood Street. A corner of I. M. Pei's City Hall is visible to the left, behind the library.

On its first try, Dallas was turned down, on the grounds that its economy was too healthy. But Mayor Robert Folsom and other city officials traveled to Washington and lobbied for changes in the enabling legislation, arguing that while Dallas did have low unemployment, there were pockets of unemployment that would benefit from the project. As a result, Dallas was awarded \$5.3 million in August 1977, \$4.9 million of which was earmarked for the new library.[2]

The city was prepared to allocate between \$25 and \$28 million to the project in the next bond proposal, but this would still leave the library about \$10 million short. However, two major gifts indicated that private funds might be available. In 1975 Virginia Lazenby O'Hara, a longtime member of the Friends of the Dallas Public Library, died and left \$1.8 million for a fine books area in the proposed central library. And in January 1977, Mr. and Mrs. Edmund J. Kahn donated \$3 million in stock for acquisition of books, tapes, films, recordings, periodicals, and other library materials for the new library, on conditions that it be similar in size, scope, and purpose to the plans outlined by Fisher and Spillman and that it be built by 1982.[3] "Eddie Kahn in particular was a strong supporter of libraries," recalled Richard Waters, Associate Director for Public Services, who oversaw construction of the new Central Library. "He and his wife were so generous to the library in many ways, but this donation was an especially important challenge, because it helped accelerate the process."[4]

Civic leaders, therefore, conceived of what was then an innovative concept—a public-private partnership to raise funds for a major public building. The $4.9 million in federal funds and $25 to $28 million in city bond money would be combined with $10 million raised from the private sector. In April 1977, former Mayor J. Erik Jonsson, now seventy-five years old and largely retired from public life, agreed to head the solicitation committee. "I've always felt that education really has its beginnings in books," Jonsson explained. "I've lived with them all my life, and I want to help make them available to everybody who needs them, who will use them. I've said all along that I would help any way I could in getting the new downtown library built—and now I'm ready to do so."[5] According to Lillian Bradshaw, Jonsson "wanted to educate everybody to be a better citizen," and he saw the public library as an essential instrument in achieving this goal. "Like Cleora Clanton," observed Mrs. Bradshaw, "Mr. Jonsson was indomitable in sticking up for what he wanted." And he was willing to put his money behind his beliefs.[6] During the next few months, Jonsson appealed to business leaders and foundation officials throughout the area, calling in "chits" he had earned in his decades of civic activity. Mrs. Bradshaw accompanied him on many of the calls, operating a slide projector with images of the architects' designs.[7] At groundbreaking ceremonies in December, Jonsson was able to report that he had collected nearly half the donations needed. His personal goal was $10 to $15 million. He also made it clear that he didn't want the library project to take as long as City Hall. "It has been twelve years since the original architect's contract was let for the City Hall, and municipal workers are only just now moving in," the former mayor complained. "I haven't got the time to wait

When this aerial photograph was taken, the site subsequently occupied by the Central Library was a parking lot. Construction was just beginning on City Hall.

that long for the completion of the central research library."[8] The new library was, in fact, proceeding on a "fast track" process, under which construction took place in steps as funding became available. This was why groundbreaking ceremonies were held before all the money was in hand.

On June 10, 1978, voters approved Proposition 2 of the bond issue, which provided $27.04 million for construction of the Central Library, as well as one new branch library (in Northwest Oak Cliff) and acquisition of sites for three more branches. This vote of confidence was enhanced by the fact that voters turned down six of the seventeen proposals, including ones for a new art museum and a new concert hall.[9] And by December, Erik Jonsson had secured $12 million in private contributions. Major commitments came from Dallas foundations, such as Hoblitzelle, Fikes, and McDermott. Entire floors were underwritten by donors, as were meeting rooms and lecture halls.

Meanwhile, the library staff began preparing for life in a state-of-the-art facility. Antoinette Johnson, librarian for systems development, began work in 1973 to computerize the card catalog, utilizing an in-house system developed by City of Dallas programmers. She and her staff spent two years inventorying every book, record, picture, magazine, and tape shelved anywhere in the stacks of the downtown library or the eighteen branches. New acquisitions were entered into the computer as they arrived. By 1981 the system was being tested at the newest branches—Oak Lawn and Highland Hills—with volunteers helping patrons learn to use the computer terminals. Like libraries throughout the country, Mrs. Bradshaw explained,

Former Mayor J. Erik Jonsson, who headed private fundraising efforts for the new Central Library, wielded the shovel at groundbreaking ceremonies in December 1977.

The library's first computer contained a database for The New York Times.

the Dallas Public Library now viewed itself as a "public information resource center" that stored information in new ways and made it available to the public more quickly. Books would never be obsolete, but audio-visual materials such as films and records now represented twenty percent of the library's holdings. The Audelia Road branch library started a pilot program offering videotapes of movies and cartoons. Plans for the downtown library even included a television production studio linked to the city's new cable TV system.[10]

The old Commerce Street library closed in March 1982, and the staff began packing for the move to the new building. (Expenses of the move were to be funded by the sale of the old building.)[11] In a month they were settled, and the Central Dallas Public Library was dedicated April 18, followed by a week of special programs, exhibits, and activities. The new library included a 200-seat auditorium and a Community Showcase exhibit area on the plaza level. Patrons could access the collections through eighty computer terminals donated by Texas Instruments. Computers also linked users to more than 200 databases in the areas of science, business, education, humanities, and the social sciences. Among the small, innovative features of the building was a room on the third floor, named for Dallas author Frances Mossiker, reserved for writers. Here a serious scholar could work undisturbed and leave research materials overnight.[12] Other study areas and conference and meeting rooms were available on different floors.

Another innovation was The Library Store, which sold products made especially for the Dallas Public Library as well as toys,

Dallas Mayor Robert Folsom and former mayors Wes Wise, Erik Jonsson, and Jack Evans participated in dedication ceremonies for the new Central Library on April 18, 1982.

The Young Street façade of the new Central Library presented a pleasing counterpoint to City Hall across the street.

games, greeting cards, and boutique items from other libraries, museums, and commercial concerns. Located on the first floor and staffed primarily by volunteers—mostly members of the Junior League and the National League of Jewish Women, but also unaffiliated individuals—The Library Store was quite successful in earning additional revenue for the library.[13]

"It turned out to be a very good building," recalled Associate Director Richard Waters. "The only thing we didn't anticipate properly was the traffic pattern in and out of the main floor. We expected patrons to enter through one set of security gates and exit through another, but within the first five minutes after the library opened, one person turned around and tried to go back out the entry gates. So we had to modify them." Otherwise, everything worked with remarkable smoothness.[14]

Originally those planning the new building had wanted to call it the Central Research Library, reflecting the fact that most of its floors would be devoted to collections in depth, staffed with specialists, offering a kind of service not available in the branches. A city councilman, however, found the concept of a "Research Library" confusing and so, according to Mrs. Bradshaw, the word "Research" was dropped from the title.[15] In 1986 it was renamed in honor of the man who had spearheaded the campaign to build it, and it became the J. Erik Jonsson Central Library.[16]

Unlike Cleora Clanton, Lillian Bradshaw was able to move into and enjoy the new library building she had worked so many years to achieve. But her directorship was drawing to a close. She was already sixty-seven years old when the new building opened. She was beginning to

The ground-floor auditorium in the new Central Library seats 200 people.

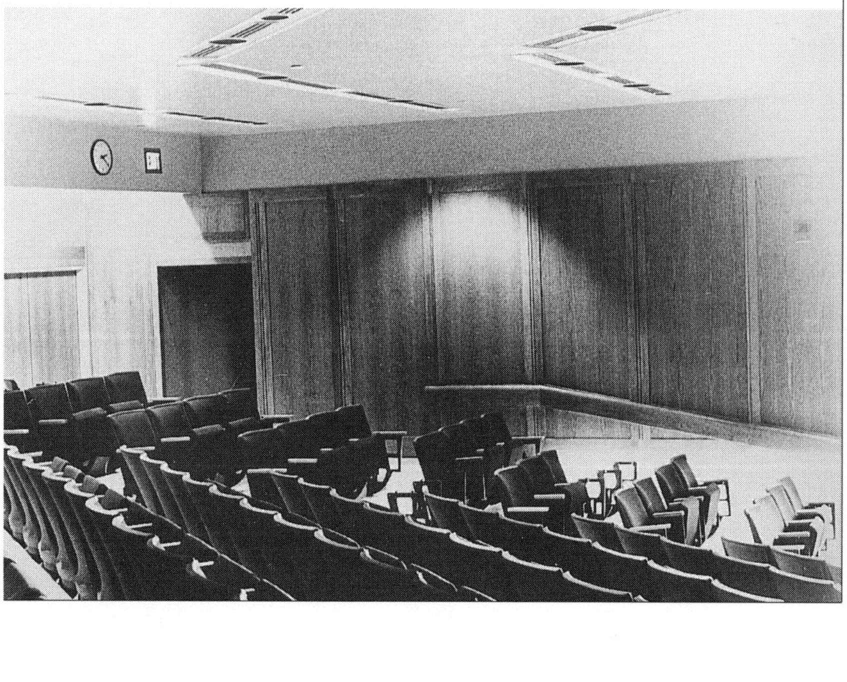

consider retirement, although, as she noted the next year, "Every time I reach a decision, something else exciting comes along." In April 1983, the City Council appointed her to work six months as special coordinator of the municipal courts system, which was experiencing backlogs in jury trials, outstanding warrants, and appeal bonds.[17] She completed the assignment in November and scheduled her retirement as library director for February 1, 1984. The next day she moved across the street to City Hall to become assistant to City Manager Charles Anderson for the 1984 Republican National Convention in Dallas. "She's one of the finest managers with whom I've worked," Anderson said. "She's well-respected and she gets things done. Lillian wasn't ready to quit. She wants some meaningful work to do. She responded enthusiastically to my request."[18]

Local technology pioneer Texas Instruments, in which Erik Jonsson was a principal, donated eighty computers for the new Central Library, making it one of the first public libraries in the country with a computerized catalog.

During her distinguished twenty-two-year career as head of the Dallas Public Library, Mrs. Bradshaw served as president of both the Texas Library Association (1964-65) and the American Library Association (1971-72). Several universities bestowed honorary doctorates on her, and Texas Woman's University created an endowed chair in library science in her name. In 1975 she was a finalist for Librarian of Congress but asked that her name be withdrawn because she preferred to remain in Dallas. "I prefer people-to-people work," she explained, "and that is what the Dallas library system is all about."[19] Although she dealt very competently with the many administrative responsibilities of her job as library director—budgets, personnel matters, raising funds—it was her personal touch that endeared Mrs. Bradshaw to all who

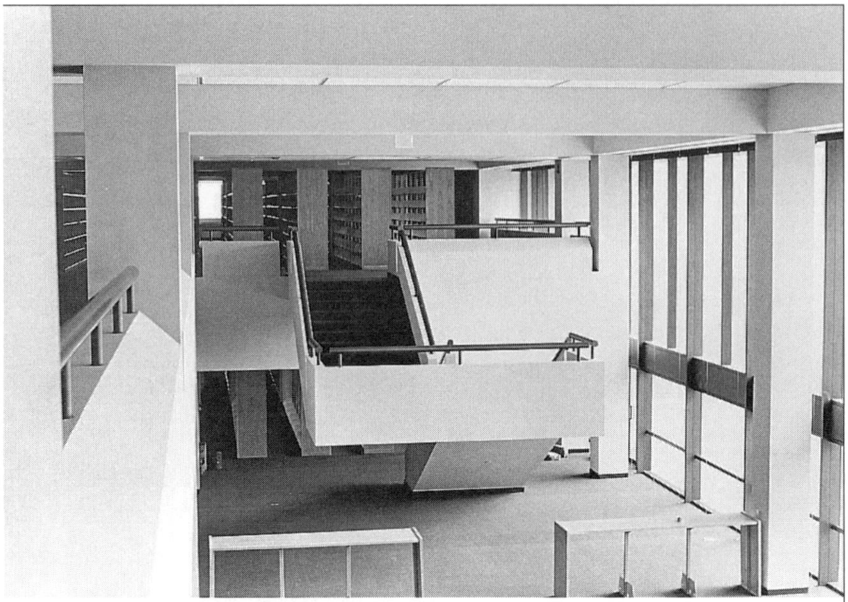

A stairway between the fifth and sixth floors of the new Central Library typified the contemporary lines of the building.

came into contact with her. "I used to walk through the library with her," recalled Charlotte Geary, who served as chair of the library board during part of Mrs. Bradshaw's tenure, "and she called every person who worked there by name. She would say, 'How is your mother doing?' or 'How is the baby?' She knew something about everybody." Her warmth was a great asset in dealing with the city bureaucracy. "She got along beautifully with the people at City Hall," Mrs. Geary said. "She had the ability to get her point of view over, but she never minced words. She was very direct, but direct in a charming way."[20] George Schrader, who was city manager during Mrs. Bradshaw's first nine years as library director, described her as "a take-charge director who would not be denied." "Lillian could have run the fire department, the police department or any other department," he said. "I tell her sometimes that *I* was working for *her* all those years."[21]

Richard Waters, the Associate Librarian for Public Services, served as acting director for six months while the city conducted a search for a permanent head. Patrick O'Brien, forty-one, became the sixth director of the Dallas Public Library on July 28, 1984. O'Brien came to Dallas from Ohio, where for five years he had been executive director of the public library system for Cuyahoga County, serving the forty-nine communities surrounding the city of Cleveland. He had previously worked as assistant commissioner for the Central Library and Cultural Center in Chicago and as chief of reference for Newsweek Magazine Editorial Library. He held two master's degrees, in library science from the University of Rhode Island, Kingston, and in business administration from Case Western Reserve in Cleveland. Mrs. Bradshaw expressed enthusiasm over the choice of O'Brien as her successor. "You have professional experience that is recognized nationally. You have a personal approach to public librarianship, friendliness, openness, an ability to respond to the needs of people. I really think the selection committee did a terrific job of selecting the right person for the community." O'Brien was equally complimentary in his remarks about Mrs. Bradshaw. "I'm certainly trying to carry on a tradition and dedication to excellence in library service that she had. What she left is a tremendous base to continue to grow upon."[22]

Among O'Brien's goals was the creation of a friendly, welcoming atmosphere in the library. Visitors should be greeted when they entered and assisted in finding what they needed. "They ought to feel that if the information is anywhere in the system, that person will find it," he explained.[23] Within a year O'Brien transformed the first floor of the Central Library, which had been somewhat stark, into "a downtown branch library," by moving the Current Collection—comprising recent fiction and nonfiction—there and displaying it in a bookstore fashion. "We want to turn it into a people place," he said.[24] Later in 1985 O'Brien carried the bookstore concept further by opening BookEnds as an expansion of The Library Store, offering thousands of books no longer needed by the library. "We've always had to remove books one way or another—every library has—in order to make room for more and better information," explained June Leftwich, the Manager of Volunteer/Enterprise Programs. "It is far bet-

Local historian A. C. Greene, left, and Charlotte Geary, longtime library benefactor, right, were among those saluting Lillian Bradshaw, center, in January 1984, on her retirement after twenty-two years as director of the Dallas Public Library.

ter that we sell these books and the revenue come back to us so we may buy more books." All revenue earned at BookEnds, in fact, was earmarked for buying library materials—not the general budget—and most of the staff were volunteers. Leftwich saw the used book store offering good support for the library's mission in another way: "Any time you can encourage reading, book ownership, the love of books," she said, "you have encouraged library usage."[25]

In 1985 O'Brien also announced plans to develop a new children's area. Use of the old Commerce Street library by children had declined during its last decade, and so planners had not anticipated much need for a children's area in the new building. The small third-floor area designated for children's literature was really for adults studying children's literature, not children. But the excitement surrounding the opening of the new Central Library began to draw families back downtown, and O'Brien was anxious to build on their interest. With the current books collection moved from the second floor to the lobby level, O'Brien proposed to turn the now-empty 7,500-square-foot area on the second floor into "a full-blown children's center," complete with a puppet theater, a read-aloud room, a computer bank, and a video-electronics area. Over the grand staircase leading from the ground floor, O'Brien envisioned "a big arrow or something, maybe in neon, saying 'Kids'." Renovation costs would be $225,000 to $250,000, to be raised from private donations.[26]

Patrick O'Brien became director of the Dallas Public Library in July 1984. Expanding the Central Library's children's area was one of his early goals.

The Dallas Public Library seemed to be enjoying unprecedented success. During the 1984-85 fiscal year, 4,081,187 items were checked out of the

Hard-working volunteers staffed BookEnds, the library's used book store, which opened in 1985.

central and branch libraries, an increase of more than five percent over the previous year. Library cards issued to individuals rose to nearly 130,000, a seven percent increase, while company cards jumped to 1,315, a 56.2 percent increase. To keep pace with the rising demand, the library announced several new projects for 1986: branch libraries would open in the fall in North Oak Cliff and Far North Dallas, and the library would conduct its first used book sale April 18-20 on the plaza in front of the Central Library. The sale of 30,000 books would coincide with an International Bazaar being held downtown.[27]

The library also received a very special gift at the beginning of 1986. To mark its one hundredth anniversary, the Dallas Shakespeare Club donated a rare first folio edition of Shakespeare's plays. The book was one of about 200 remaining copies of an edition printed in 1623, seven years after the playwright's death. It was displayed on the first floor of the Central Library in a secured, climate-controlled case donated by the Friends of the Dallas Public Library.[28] Later it was moved to a specially designed room on the seventh floor, near the rare books area. The fact that Mrs. Henry Exall, the first president of the Dallas Library Association, had also been the first president of the Dallas Shakespeare Club (serving in that position for fifty years) provided an appropriate historic footnote to the proceedings.

By the summer of 1986, as Patrick O'Brien marked his second anniversary as director, the Dallas Public Library had risen to new heights, not only in traditional areas such as circulation, but in innovative fields as well. Its cable television programs, for instance, were enjoying great success, particularly interviews with authors, who loved chatting with librarians who had actually read their books. Through these programs, the library was building a valuable network with publishers and gaining some national acclaim.[29] As Shakespeare himself might have warned, however, success seldom continues unchallenged, and disaster often waits ahead. The Dallas economy had experienced a phenomenal boom during the past decade, with so much construction that the crane had been jokingly declared the city's bird. But beginning in the mid-1980s, declining world petroleum prices hit the city's oil-dependent economy hard. Real estate foreclosures began to proliferate. Texas banks experienced a dramatic turndown caused by overextension of bank credit, and by loose lending to energy and energy-related fields and commercial real estate developers. Seven of the ten largest commercial banks in Texas failed between 1987 and 1990. The city saw its tax base shrinking. City officials began to look for ways to cut the municipal budget.

The Dallas Public Library was about to enter perhaps the most traumatic period of its history.

Chapter 12

A Library Under Siege

In May 1986 City Manager Charles Anderson instructed library administrators to cut the budget three percent, effective June 1. This amounted to $500,000. Patrick O'Brien responded by delaying the opening of the two new branch libraries and temporarily closing the fine arts listening center. Library employees received pay cuts ranging from one to three percent—as did all city employees. While staff morale was affected by the pay cuts, O'Brien praised the librarians for "bearing up very well." Like most city employees, he added, "their concern is what happens next."[1]

Their concern was justified. A few weeks later, O'Brien was ordered to lop $1.5 million from the library's 1986-87 budget. His biggest proposed cut ($416,000) was removal of the public access computer terminals. "This is a giant setback technologically for us," O'Brien announced. "Ours is the first urban public library in twenty-five years that opened without a card catalog and provides total access to the collection." The computers would be replaced by a microfiche system that would increase the time required to find a book and would mean a three-month lag in posting new holdings. Other proposed cuts included $23,000 in the library's community services department and $64,000 in book binding. In addition, approximately forty-eight staff members would lose their jobs, the Central Library would no longer be open evenings, and two branch libraries (Dallas West and Park Forest) would be closed. "No city institution, including the library, should be exempt from the belt tightening that budget problems demand," admitted Phil Seib, chairman of the board of the Friends of the Dallas Public Library. "But all the public officials so intent on scurrying for cover while the budget storm rages should keep in mind that they are cutting not fat, but the intellectual marrow of the city."[2]

Anita Martinez, the first Mexican-American to serve on the Dallas City Council, sponsored a troupe of folklorico dancers that brought Hispanic culture to the library. This performance was at the Dallas West Branch.

By early August O'Brien was being ordered to recommend cuts of $3 million (twenty percent) in the library's $16 million budget. Facing a $47 million shortfall in revenue, but terrified to raise taxes, the City Council had instructed City Manager Anderson to present a budget that retained the city's current tax rate, and he was wielding the ax across the board, affecting all city departments. The proposed retrenchment in library services created a public uproar and resulted in petitions, calls, and letters to City Council members. The proposed closing of the Dallas West branch library, for instance, spurred the collection of petitions with more than 2,500 signatures. Selected for closure because it had the lowest number of users in the library system, Dallas West nevertheless served a lower-class neighborhood where most parents couldn't afford to buy books, magazines, or newspapers for their children. Dallas West also had the largest collection of Spanish-language materials in the library system.[3] Distinguished Texas historian T. R. Fehrenbach leant his support at the library's first Literary Lions Dinner in September. "Most politicians in Texas don't understand the importance of public libraries to poor children," Fehrenbach told the black-tie audience, whose financial support

The Friends of the Dallas Public Library launched an annual Literary Lions Dinner in 1986, with initial proceeds benefiting the Central Library's new children's area.

was pledged to benefit the Central Library's new children's section. "If our children and their children are going to be literate, we must begin to appreciate what we have here."[4]

Public outcry saved the two branches from closing, and the computer terminals were not removed, but the library still endured reduced hours and services, as well as staff layoffs and pay cuts. The branch libraries had to cut seventeen hours from their weekly operations, magazine subscriptions were reduced by twenty-five percent, and thousands fewer books were ordered. At the same time, like the Great Depression, the economic downturn resulted in record crowds swamping the library, creating long lines at check-out counters and a shortage of books on subjects ranging from resume writing to bankruptcy. One newspaper with job listings, *The National Business Employment Weekly*, became so popular that reference librarians had to require patrons to leave identification to ensure that the paper would be returned. "A lot of people are checking out self-help books on how to go about a job search, how to write a resume, how to write a business letter and such," Patrick O'Brien explained. "Lots of people are also deciding to spend Sunday afternoon at the Central Library instead of at the shopping mall." The number of items checked out at the Central Library in February 1987 was up 9.5 percent over the same month in 1986, and up 6.8 percent at the branch libraries.[5] The increased use of the libraries only emphasized the cutbacks in service.

Another round of budget cuts in 1987 reduced the library's purchase of materials more than $400,000, meaning that 25,000 books never made it to the library shelves. The library also closed its 16 mm. film library, stopped six hours of weekly library pro-

Library Director Patrick O'Brien, left, and City Councilman Bill Milkie participated in groundbreaking ceremonies for the North Oak Cliff Branch Library in 1986.

The Renner-Frankford Branch Library opened in 1986.

gramming of cable television, permanently closed the listening center where records could be previewed before being checked out, reduced the number of exhibits, stopped lunchtime programs at the Central Library, and curtailed most of its community outreach programs, including adult education. The library began charging patrons one dollar to reserve a book, and it doubled fees for nonresidents. The library even stopped sending notices for overdue books, although the amount saved in postage was offset by a more than $40,000 drop in fine receipts. These cuts were made, O'Brien pointed out, at a time when use of the library was the highest in five years.[6] Among the few bright notes were the openings of the North Oak Cliff and Renner Frankford branch libraries early in 1987—delayed for several months because there wasn't enough money in the budget to staff them. Both were state-of-the-art facilities, well designed to fit into their surroundings.[7]

The library's management team found itself bonding as it coped with the continual directives to cut expenditures. Most of the managers had come up through the ranks (many had been branch managers), and felt a sense of investment in the system. They had to prepare budgets that cut five or ten percent of the staff, never knowing if the cuts would be fully enacted. "It was a gut-wrenching ordeal," observed one assistant director. "We did the best we could under the circumstances."[8] Division heads faced their own frustrations. Hundreds of high school and college students, for instance, visited the Humanities Division in the Central Library to conduct research for papers. The division had developed a strong collection of scholarly journals, in some cases dating back decades. Now it was forced to cancel many of its subscriptions. It could no longer afford to duplicate material, or replace damaged or lost books. Often it couldn't add new works of literary criticism to its collection, a "very painful" process, recalled division head Frances Bell, because such books didn't stay in print long, and the Dallas Library had probably lost them forever. The Humanities Division also cut back on the number of copies of current fiction it acquired, causing much disappointment among patrons. And of course, with staff cuts, fewer people were doing more work with fewer resources.[9]

A special kind of patron, homeless individuals, had found a haven at the downtown library for years, but by the summer of 1987 their numbers seemed to be increasing dramatically. A mayoral committee estimated that as many as 14,000 people in Dallas were without a home. Destitute, sometimes mentally ill, these unfortunate individuals were drawn to the downtown area by soup kitchens and overnight shelters. Dallas, however, offered no day shelters, and the public library was one of the few buildings within walking distance where the homeless felt safe and relatively welcome. The problem was their impact on regular patrons. When the doors opened at 9 A.M., several dozen homeless people would scurry to the bathrooms to wash up and shave. They would then stretch out for hours in comfortable reading chairs, occasionally dozing. Even during mild weather, 100 to 200 homeless people could usually be found sitting or sleeping in the library; in poor weather, the number often doubled. Regular patrons, forced to share an elevator with a street person, or unable to find a

A young book lover finds an array of offerings at the library's annual used book sale.

June Leftwich, Manager of Volunteer/Enterprise Programs for the library, sorts books to be included in the library's first used book sale, April 18-20, 1986. (Photo courtesy of The Dallas Morning News. *Photo by Paula Nelson)*

quiet place to sit because the chairs were occupied, began to complain. "The most frequent complaint I get is about street people," O'Brien told a reporter. "And the complaints are usually about the way they smell." The library was being forced to deal with a problem the city was reluctant to approach. O'Brien had appealed to the Greater Dallas Commission for the Homeless for help. "This is not a library problem or a City Hall problem," O'Brien said. "It's a citywide problem that needs to be solved by a coalition of groups. We all need to work together to take the burden off the library."[10] The following March the city finally opened a Day Resource Center, which eased the library's burden. But in the meantime it was forced to enact a series of new "Rules of Behavior" that banned bathing, shaving, or washing clothes in the building, bringing in bedrolls or blankets, gambling, and panhandling.[11] These were the 1980s version of the 1901 rules that restricted use of the library to people "of good deportment, character and habits."

As the Dallas economy continued to plummet, the library endured more budget cuts. Often, without warning, book budgets would be frozen, meaning nothing could be bought until the end of the budget year. Librarians began to be seriously concerned about the long-term effect of the reduced book budget on the collections. The Dallas Public Library was spending less than eleven percent of its budget on books, while standard practice among good libraries called for at least fifteen percent. "Irreparable harm" could be done, cautioned O'Brien, "because most books are on the market for only a short time, so even an expanded budget some years down the road won't ensure that the library will be able to recoup its losses." Ironically, in the fall of 1987 the Dallas Public Library was selected as the site for the Texas Center for the Book, the only Texas library so designated by the Library of Congress. Its status would enable the Dallas library to expand its programming by taking advantage of technical assistance from the Library of Congress, as well as benefiting from private donations earmarked for the center's work. "The center will bring to Dallas things that we alone would not be able to do," explained O'Brien, "such as sponsoring a major literary festival." Traveling exhibits would now be more likely to visit Dallas, and the center could engineer cooperative ventures among libraries throughout the state. The center was "a logical extension of library activity," O'Brien said, "but it's much bigger than a library, because it celebrates everything a book is, from art object to information provider."[12]

In April 1988 the Dallas City Council issued a proclamation declaring April 17-23, which was National Library Week, as Dallas Public Library Appreciation Week. Phil Seib, a columnist for *The Dallas Morning News* and the outgoing chairman of the Friends of the Dallas Public Library, found the proclamation sadly ironic. "The same City Council that is so lavish in the rhetoric of its proclamation," he wrote, "is presiding over the demise of an institution crucial to Dallas's future." Seib pointed out that since 1985 the library's budget had dropped more than fifteen percent. During the past ten years its buying power had been cut by forty-six percent. A smaller staff was overseeing twice as much space and four times as large a collection as it had in

A "Pied Piper" leads the way to the Central Library's new Children's Center at the grand opening in May 1989.

1982. But library supporters were organizing to fight back. A group called Citizens for Library Excellence was mounting a low-budget but high-energy lobbying effort (paid for by the Friends of the Dallas Public Library, Inc.) to remind the City Council how much libraries meant to Dallas. Its members gave speeches to civic groups, encouraged letter writing to City Council members, and recruited people to attend town hall meetings and budget hearings.[13]

Librarian Marianne Satarino answers questions for patrons of the new Children's Center on the second floor of the Central Library.

Volunteers were working hard on other fronts, too. The library's first three used book sales (in April and October 1986 and April 1987), along with proceeds from BookEnds, netted about $125,000, all of which went into the acquisitions fund. The fourth book sale, in April 1988, was the largest yet, with more than 40,000 books available.[14] The Friends of the Dallas Public Library continued with its successful Literary Lions gala, inaugurated in 1986, by bringing Robert Caro, N. Scott Momaday, Shirley Ann Grau, and J. California Cooper to Dallas in October 1988. In addition to raising $30,000 at the gala, the Friends also presented the authors in a free, public, noontime reading at the Central Library.[15] And the citizens of Dallas continued to demonstrate their support of and need for the public library by setting new records for use. In the fiscal year that ended September 30, 1988, patrons checked out 4,237,153 books, and 120,543 citizens got new library cards, bringing the total to more than 300,000 people.[16]

During the fall of 1988, after raising $350,000, the library was finally able to begin construction on the new children's center, the dream Patrick O'Brien had been pursuing for nearly four years.[17] At the heart of the 11,000-square-foot space was a computer area where

Dan Foote's editorial cartoon captured the frustration of Dallas residents who saw budget cuts eroding library service.

children could use software programs to help improve their reading skills. "Something has to be done to break the cycle of kids dropping out of school and adult illiteracy," O'Brien explained. "Dallas, in particular, is only now coming to recognize that the problem is as great as it is. We think the best chance is to get children while they're young and open up their horizons." "Reading is the foundation for everything you do in life."[18]

At the grand opening in May 1989, children were greeted with a colorful space with areas for every age, from toddlers to teens. Younger children could explore a village of small buildings, featuring a moat, a drawbridge, and a clock tower; preschool picture books were housed in shelves shaped like buildings. The "story-telling forest" was a transformation, through clever lighting and design, of an odd-shaped corner of the building into a lush grove with wavy walls and a sloping floor. The Kahn Pavilion (named for benefactor Edmund J. Kahn) seated about fifty children for puppet shows, skits, and other performances. Shelved throughout the children's area were 100,000 books, many of which had long been stored in closed stacks because the library had no place to put them out. A special feature—and one of the few areas open to adults unaccompanied by children—was the Siddie Joe Johnson collection of historical children's literature. Named for the beloved former head of the children's department, the collection of rare books was open to anyone researching children's literature. The children's center was divided from the rest of the second floor by glass walls featuring black-and-white photo etchings of real children interspersed with colorful graphics of historical and imaginary figures. The information desk was laminated in turquoise, while adjoining file cabinets were purple. A circle of red neon hung above the computer table. And wavy red neon lights framed the stage. "We want this to be a place where kids' imaginations can roam," explained O'Brien. "It's going to knock people's socks off," and indeed it did.[19]

The opening of the children's center brought O'Brien the city manager's first Servant as Leader Award, saluting his "ability to be a dreamer of great dreams and bring them to reality." O'Brien generously shared credit with his staff, noting that despite the budgetary constraints, the city's librarians had continued to "provide the best reading, for the largest number, at the least cost."[20]

His award was small comfort to O'Brien in September, when once again he had to fight the city's attempt to cut the library budget. "This library was intended to be one of the premier public libraries in the country," O'Brien stated. "You're not a premier public library if you nickel and dime your collection. . . . We're buying fewer books than we were ten years ago." Staffing continued to be a problem. "Our staff is working at skeletal levels everywhere," O'Brien pointed out. "We're having a recruiting problem. We are no longer competitive in the market for librarians because of salary cuts." Yet, for the fifth consecutive year, the Dallas Public Library set records in visitors and circulation.[21] Public outcry kept the library budget intact—although still thirteen percent less than it had been five years earlier—and the City Council voted $216,315 to expand hours at the Central Library, allowing it to be open Tuesday and Thursday evenings as well as Monday and Wednesday; it would also be open Sunday afternoon. The library appeared to have a new champion in the city's first elected woman mayor, Annette Strauss, who pledged, "No longer will this library be dark at night. . . . It's time to open the doors of a brighter library for a brighter future for Dallas."[22]

But even Mayor Strauss was powerless to halt the continued stagnation of the Dallas economy. Faced with a $2 billion loss of property values on the tax rolls, the city manager was instructed to look for more places to cut the budget. The library budget submitted to the city council in September 1990 proposed trimming $700,000 from staff expenditures and another $300,000 from the book and periodicals fund. An editorial in *The Dallas Morning News* pointed out that "the downtown library today is only a shadow of the one that was envisioned" a decade earlier. "Gone are the cable television studio, oral history programs, and film library. The Jonsson library should be open six nights a week.

Sandy Melton, left, headed the Friends of the Dallas Public Library from 1989 to 1992.

Instead, it is open only four nights, and the branch libraries remain open just two nights." The City Council, the editorial urged, "must decide whether some budget cuts do far more damage than the temporary tax savings they provide . . . A strong city needs a strong public library system."[23] Citizen protests mitigated the cuts but couldn't eliminate them entirely.

Like a nightmare that kept recurring, in 1991 the city manager again recommended cuts to the library budget, this time half a million dollars, mostly in staff positions. In desperation, O'Brien proposed restructuring the library system to transform thirteen of the nineteen branch libraries into "popular libraries," from which reference materials would be removed and children's programs eliminated. The alternative, he warned, would be to close the branches entirely.[24] This announcement got people's attention. "There is an outpouring of outrage from this community the likes of which I've never seen," stated Freda Gail Stern, head of Citizens for Library Excellence. More than 200 people packed a town hall meeting held by City Councilman Jerry Bartos, dozens of them speaking in support of the library. City Council members Dr. Charles Tandy in Oak Cliff and Max Wells in Far North Dallas encountered similar crowds. "People have come out of the woodwork," reported Sandy Melton, president of the Friends of the Dallas Public Library. "I thought I would have to be out there doing more. But it's apparent the citizens know the value of the library and are willing to go out and do more."[25] *The Dallas Morning News* again championed the library. "The City Council cannot allow this financial slide to continue," the editors proclaimed. "The citizens of this community have shown through

The Dallas Public Library celebrated its ninetieth birthday on October 20, 1991, with the opening of "The American Journalist: Paradox of the Press," a Library of Congress exhibit. Cutting the birthday cake were Burl Osborne, publisher of The Dallas Morning News*; Sandy Melton, president of the Friends of the Dallas Public Library; Patrick O'Brien, library director; and Charlene Howell, vice-chairman of the Municipal Library Advisory Board.*

their strong attendance that public libraries are a vital part of their lives. And in times when the rate of illiteracy here is reaching frightening proportions, further library cuts send the worst possible message."[26]

The public outcry persuaded the City Council to restore the $500,000 to the library's budget. But the effects of the annual blood-letting were costing the library experienced staff members. Susan Schmidt, manager of the Park Forest branch, left for a job in Maryland. "Every summer I wondered if I would have a job in the new fiscal year," she explained. "I watched the hours being changed, book budgets being eroded, and services being cut because we didn't have staff. I didn't want to stay in an area that didn't support libraries." Richard Miller, manager of the Oak Lawn branch, left after ten years with the Dallas system for a job in publishing. "I agonized over my decision to leave," he said, but his resignation was hastened by the city government's attitude toward the libraries, which he called "totally uncaring" and "an embarrassment."[27]

The Dallas Public Library thus celebrated its ninetieth anniversary with less exuberance than it might have wished. For the occasion it presented a major exhibition from the Library of Congress entitled "The American Journalist: Paradox of the Press." Sponsored locally by the Texas Center for the Book, the Friends of the Dallas Public Library, and *The Dallas Morning News*, the exhibit featured 250 items, including pencil drawings made on the battlefields of the Civil War, Ernie Pyle's World War II typewriter, and Bob Woodward's spiral notebook recording the Watergate break-in.[28] Patrick O'Brien took the opportunity of the anniversary to visit with *Morning News* Viewpoints editor Carolyn Barta about the challenges facing the library. City officials were too inclined to view the library as a nonessential service, whose budget could be cut "temporarily" during hard times. In fact, the library needed to be investing more, not less, as it prepared to meet the demands of the electronic age. O'Brien reported that a Price Waterhouse management audit of the library estimated that it needed to spend $3 million to purchase a new computer system, and that it would cost half a million dollars a year to operate. "To position ourselves through the 1990s," O'Brien explained, "we should be spending $2.5 to $3 million a year; instead we're spending $1.7 million." The library was currently formulating a $5 million campaign to fund the new system. However, O'Brien warned, "people don't want to give money to the library if public support is diminished."[29]

In February 1992, faced with the prospect of a decline of $14.5 million in sales tax revenue, the city manager proposed across-the-board cuts of seven percent in all departments except police and fire. "We just don't have any place to give anymore," exclaimed O'Brien. "Basically, we're nothing but books and information and people." Hours would be trimmed, and staff would be asked to work four hours less a week—a ten percent reduction—and take a ten percent cut in pay.[30]

O'Brien himself had had enough. In July he announced that he was resigning to become director of the library system in Alexandria, Virginia. He graciously explained that he and his family wanted to move back to the East Coast to be closer to his aging parents in Rhode Island. "I would be dishonest if I said there weren't times of great frustration," he admitted. "But there was also jubilation, particularly when people would come out and say, 'We love our library.'"[31] A *Dallas Morning News* editorial issued a challenge to city officials: "Along with the selection of the next director should be a promise to give books and learning the priority they have always deserved at Dallas City Hall."[32]

Chapter 13

Recovery

When Patrick O'Brien resigned as director, the Dallas Public Library was serving nearly 3 million visitors a year. According to a survey conducted by the *Dallas Business Journal*, this meant that the library was the third most popular attraction in the city, just behind the West End Marketplace and the State Fair of Texas. Some 355,212 people and 3,850 businesses held library cards. Among these, 2,773 suburban residents were willing to pay ten dollars to one hundred dollars for check-out privileges. The library's annual budget was about $14.2 million, fifteen percent less than it had been eight years earlier. [1]

Advertising the director's position at $65,000, the city found it difficult to fill. Comparable cities were paying $85,000 to more than $100,000. David Morgan, the head of the city's computer department, filled in as acting director. In the summer of 1993 he was pleased to report that many of the eighty-two positions vacant at the start of the year had been filled, that ground had been broken for a new branch library in Southwest Oak Cliff, and that $500,000 had been added to the materials budget through savings in salaries and other accounts. Especially significant, the library had developed plans for its much-needed new automation system. "I don't take credit for any of these projects," Morgan wrote library employees, "but I take lots of

Laura Welch Bush, a former librarian, was an active member of the Friends of the Dallas Public Library while her family lived in Dallas, serving as Assistant Secretary of the Board in 1993–94. Here she and her daughters, Barbara and Jenna, and her husband, George W. Bush, admire a tree in the library decorated with ornaments that previously had graced the White House Christmas tree. Mrs. Bush arranged the loan of the ornaments through her in-laws, then President George Bush and First Lady Barbara Bush.

Tommy Joe Johnson, president of the Woods/Sugarberry Neighborhood Association; Mark Housewright, Municipal Library Advisory Board member; Eloise Sherman, Municipal Library Board chairman; David Morgan, Acting Library Director; and Charles Tandy, Dallas City Councilman, participate in groundbreaking ceremonies for the Mountain Creek Branch Library in 1993.

pride in all of them. Each of you deserves the credit."[2]

Ramiro S. Salazar was named the seventh director of the Dallas Public Library in July 1993 and started work September 1. As director of libraries in El Paso for the past three years, Salazar had overseen a central library and four branches. Under his leadership, two new branches and a literacy center opened, and four capital improvement projects got underway. Prior to heading the El Paso system, Salazar had been supervisor of the main library in San Antonio and director of the Eagle Pass library.[3] As the first Hispanic to head the Dallas library, Salazar brought a special sensitivity to serving the needs of citizens who traditionally did not feel comfortable using a municipal library. "I have a vision of making public libraries much more accessible to all segments of the population," he said. In El Paso he and his employees used everything from country-and-western dance lessons to a snake handler to attract patrons. These initiatives seemed to work, as visits to El Paso libraries increased by fifty-two percent during Salazar's last two years there.[4]

The challenges facing Salazar in Dallas, of course, were formidable. The budget was still less than it had been in 1985, and visits had actually decreased by seven percent, from 2.2 million in the year ending in June 1992, to 2 million in June 1993. "The first thing he has do," counseled Lillian Bradshaw, who served on the selection committee, "is to find what the citizens want in their library, and the second is to do his damnedest to get it. We need to restore the Dallas Public Library to the plateau that it held in the past on the national scene." Salazar remained optimistic. One of his priorities, he explained, would be increasing the proposed $1.2 million materials budget. "I think it can be improved," he said. "There's never enough money for materials."[5]

By April 1994 Salazar had written a strategic plan setting far-reaching targets for the end of the decade. He wanted the library to spend five dollars per resident on materials, more than triple the then current rate. (Dallas spent less than Houston, San Antonio, Detroit, and most comparable U.S. cities.) And Salazar wanted to see library cards in the hands of eighty percent of residents, doubling the number. His wish list included two grant writers on staff, to ferret out state, federal, and private funds for which the library might be eligible, but which its overburdened employees had never had the time to pursue.[6] The Friends continued to do their part by generating thousands of dollars each year to support the library. "An Evening with Barbara Bush," sponsored by the Friends in September 1994, benefited all twenty branch libraries as well as the Children's Center downtown. The presence of the former First Lady, a prominent proponent of literacy, underscored the importance of the public library system to the city.[7]

Ramiro Salazar became the seventh director of the Dallas Public Library in 1993.

Unfortunately, the city council seemed to be locked into a mindset that while police and firefighters deserved a fifteen percent pay raise—costing the city more than $60 million—the public library was of less importance. When the library asked to be included on a bond election ballot in May 1995 for $16 million, the council trimmed its request to $237,000. Yet eight branch libraries had leaking roofs, and the Preston Royal branch even had to be closed for six months when the roof caved in. Other branches had asbestos problems, malfunctioning heating and cooling systems, tattered furniture, and bad plumbing. Because of the cuts in the acquisitions budget, some reference material was badly out of date; a student doing a research report on Texas governors at one branch library could find nothing after Mark White, who left office in 1987.[8]

In a series of articles and editorials publicizing the sorry plight of the library, *The Dallas Morning News* pointed out that Dallas was hardly the only city that experienced a financial meltdown during the oil slump of the 1980s. Yet its fellow sufferers had not necessarily decimated the library budget in reaction. Denver, for instance, with half the population of Dallas, spent twice as much per capita on its library system. Its operating schedule had remained unchanged, keeping the Denver libraries open far more hours than Dallas. In 1990 Denver voters had approved $91.6 million in bond funds for the library system, including more than $70 million for a new downtown library. Denver librarian Rick Ashton attributed the public support to the fact that the city never allowed library services to deteriorate. "We've always placed a high value on books and education," Ashton explained. Despite cuts in the defense industry, Los Angeles was proceeding with plans for a new central library. Proposed reductions at the military bases around San Antonio hadn't stopped that city from opening a new downtown library. The mission for the Dallas City Council, the newspaper asserted, was clear: "They must stop the bleeding in the library system and start shoring up the wounds." The materials budget needed to be set at $3 million and increased annually. The most serious building problems should be addressed. And the library needed to develop more outreach programs for Dallas students.[9]

Former First Lady Barbara Bush, shown with her daughter-in-law (and Friends officer) Laura Bush, left, and Friends President Lillian Bradshaw, spoke at the Friends of the Dallas Public Library fundraiser in September 1994.

One bright spot was that in April 1995 the city council did

Dallas Mayor Ron Kirk presided at ceremonies for ribbon-cutting at the Library Online located on the ground floor of the Central Library in 1998.

An assortment of dignitaries, including City Councilman Al Lipscomb, far left, and Mayor Ron Kirk, second from right, snip the ribbon to open the renovated first floor of the Central Library Feb. 14, 1998.

approve replacing the library's obsolete automation system. The electronic card catalog would be upgraded, it would be easier to use (even by children), and it would allow multilingual access. Patrons would be able to dial into the on-line catalog from home. And people who didn't own personal computers could use the library's equipment to gain access to the Internet. The cost of the new system would be about $5.5 million.[10]

Even this benefit, however, was not without controversy. In order to pay for it, the city council decided to raid the library's $3.5 million endowment fund. This fund had been created in 1981 from the sale of the old Commerce Street library building, and over the years it had generated $5.6 million in interest income. City staff and most council members called it the best way to finance the new computer system, "because it was considered a luxury." But critics feared that the action would discourage potential donors by sending the signal that they couldn't trust the city to keep endowments intact. "The city council can do whatever the hell it pleases," said former director Patrick O'Brien, "but it defeats the whole purpose and intent." The director of the Tulsa, Oklahoma, Library Trust called the idea of spending principal a "dreadful situation." But the Friends of the Dallas Public Library and the Municipal Library Advisory Board reluctantly supported using the endowment for what they felt was an essential investment, as long as fifty percent of the cost came from the surplus in the city's general operating funds. This was the compromise approved by the city council.[11]

The new STAR (System to Access Resources) network officially went online in November 1996. In addition to providing

The Kleberg-Rylie Branch Library opened in 1995.

quick access to the Dallas Public Library's own collections, 287 personal computers allowed patrons to use databases in other libraries, search for periodicals, view historic photographs on-screen, and call up any Web site they wanted. Patrons could also access the STAR system from home, through a personal computer and modem. The Friends celebrated by hosting a party complete with a brass band at the Central Library, while the branches offered games, prizes, refreshments, puppet shows, films, and songs. Orientation tours and drawings for free tickets to sporting events were held at all locations.[12]

All the hoopla had a serious undertone. It was designed to get people into the library and acquaint them with STAR. In addition to freshly trained staff, a small army of volunteers from the National Council of Jewish Women was on hand to help confused patrons during the first few months. The computer terminals were actually color coded, with blue work-stations offering all services including the Internet, red "express" stations offering access only to the Dallas library's catalog, and special purple ones with cartoon animals geared to a third-grade level. Through STAR, patrons of the Dallas Public Library could finally take full advantage of the wealth of information available in the new digital age. The Dallas library, explained Freda Gail Stern, a member of the Library Advisory Board, was trying "to level the playing field, so that we may avoid becoming a society of information haves and have-nots." Ultimately, STAR would enable the Dallas library to fulfill a basic mission. "The public library is the most democratic institution we have," Ms. Stern said. "It provides literature and information to people who otherwise would have no access to them."[13]

Councilman Al Lipscomb cuts the ribbon to open the Skillman-Southwestern Branch Library in 1995.

The inauguration of STAR capped a year that had finally seen the fortunes of the Dallas Public Library improving. In January Dallas Southwest Osteopathic Physicians Inc. announced that it was awarding $25,000 to two Oak Cliff branch libraries (North Oak Cliff and Hampton-Illinois). "Our community must realize that our libraries are not luxuries, but are essential for the continued education of our youth," said Dr. J. L. LaManna, chairman of the group's board. "We need to restore the respect and acceptance that our libraries have had in the past."[14] A few months later the Eugene McDermott Foundation pledged $500,000 for major ground-floor improvements at the Central Library. The Friends of the Dallas Public Library agreed to raise an additional $500,000, and the city committed another $1 million.[15] Ramiro Salazar, who spearheaded the negotiations with private donors, saw the first floor renovations as the first step in a continuing private-public partnership to upgrade and renovate each floor of the Central Library. The renovation project included a new technology center to highlight the STAR system. Gail Bialas, the library marketing manager, described it as "something that might have made the late J. Erik Jonsson smile. He and others provided the 'push' to make Dallas Public Library the first public library in the world with its entire catalog online."[16] The most encouraging development, however, was that the library's operating budget was finally increasing, thanks to a slow but steady revival in the local economy. By 1996 the library was getting $17.6 million from the city, enough to patch some holes in the collections, if not the holes in the leaking roofs.[17]

The library system was also getting a brand new branch—at no cost. Kroger Food Stores was so anxious to acquire the site on Cedar Springs Boulevard occupied by the Oak Lawn branch that it offered to build a replacement library a few yards away and to pay for temporary quarters during construction. Although the current Oak Lawn building was only fifteen years old, its roof leaked, and its multilevel design made it awkward to get from one part of the building to another. Library Director Salazar was, therefore, happy

Dena Jones, President of the Friends of the Dallas Public Library, Inc., holds plans during renovation of the fifth floor of the Central Library for the Nancy and Jake L. Hamon Oil Resource Center.

to work with Kroger in carrying out the proposal. Oak Lawn closed its doors March 9, 1996. The branch moved ten blocks up the street, to a former furniture store, for a few months. And by October, a new, 12,900-square-foot building, all on one level, was ready for service.[18] In April 1999, the International City Management Association saluted the project by presenting its Public-Private Partnership Award to the City of Dallas.

New branches also opened at Kleberg-Rylie in 1995 and Skillman-Southwestern in 1996, bringing the total number of branches in the Dallas library system to twenty-two. By the late 1990s, however, many of the buildings housing these branches were more than twenty years old and beginning to show their age. Jane Shouse, a member of the Municipal Library Advisory Board, estimated in 1997 that sixteen of them needed major work. The Pleasant Grove library needed a new electrical system. Martin Luther King and Forest Green had roof leaks that were damaging some of the books in their collections. Beyond these maintenance problems, the branch libraries were now filling needs unexpected when they were built, Mrs. Shouse noted. They had become homework centers, teen centers, GED instruction locations, English-as-a-second-language training centers, literacy centers, citizenship instruction sites, and health fair sites. "They serve as the heart of the community," said Mrs. Shouse, "and unfortunately, the buildings were not built to accommodate those needs." The Walnut Hill branch was using an unheated bookmobile garage for its GED course, for instance, and the Hampton-Illinois branch had no classrooms. Although the library had been unsuccessful in getting these needs funded in the 1995 bond election, the Advisory Board was hopeful that it would gain a place on the next bond proposal.[19]

When the bond package was put together early in 1998, it did include about $6 million for the libraries. But most of this was slated to replace the Lancaster-Kiest branch. Built in 1964, this building was in very poor condition, and it occupied a narrow site with inadequate parking facilities. The remaining $2 million was earmarked for renovating the Audelia Road, Walnut Hill, and Dallas West branches. Some $40 million in needed repairs were left unfunded. A basic problem was that in 1993, after legal challenges and lengthy court proceedings, the city of Dallas had switched to a "14-1" council system, under which fourteen members of the City Council were elected from specific voting districts, while only the mayor was elected at large. Great attention was paid to drawing electoral districts that reflected the city's racial make-up, and each city council member was primarily concerned with looking after the interests of his or her district. When the bond proposal was put together, the total amount (excluding large-scale projects such as the Trinity River improvement program or the new basketball arena) was divided evenly among the districts. For the 1998 package, the amount was $10 million per district. Any proposed funds for repairs to a branch library in a particular district had to compete with proposals for street repairs and other projects in that district. "When a replacement library costs $4 million," explained council member Veletta Forsythe Lill, "that's a big chunk out of a single district's budget. Each member has to decide, 'Do my constituents need streets—or do they need a library?'" Ms. Lill planned to introduce a resolution that, in the future, library bonds not be broken up district by district. "My cause is to convince my colleagues that our library is a system," she said. "It's a citywide asset. Everyone benefits from the libraries, not just the people in one district."[20] Thanks in large measure to Ms. Lill's efforts, the library's portion of the bond proposal was increased to $10.5 million.[21] And the library system was indeed reclassified as a citywide asset.

Encouraging public support at the polls was the timely announcement that Dallas philanthropist Nancy Hamon had donated $1 million to renovate the fifth floor of the Central Library to create the Nancy and Jake L. Hamon Oil and Gas Resource Center. Mrs. Hamon's gift would replace worn-out carpet and furniture and install new lighting and computer workstations. It would also pay for training in the use of the Business and Technology Division housed on the fifth floor. Equally significant, given the library's history of deferred maintenance, half of the gift was earmarked for a permanent endowment to help pay for upkeep and materials for the center in the future.[22] A week later came news that the Gates Library Foundation, established by Microsoft billionaire Bill Gates and his wife, Melinda French Gates, had awarded the Dallas Public Library $160,000 to purchase fifty computer workstations. Twenty of those would form an Internet training center at the Central Library, while thirty would be divided among five branch libraries in South and West Dallas.[23]

The bond proposal passed, as nearly every such proposal that benefited the library had passed during the past seventy years. Included in the program was $350,000 for a master facilities plan for the library. The Hillier Group, a national architecture and planning consulting firm with specific expertise in libraries, was engaged to draft the plan. Joseph C. Rizzo, AIA, a principal of the firm and a specialist in library planning and design with more than forty library-related projects to his credit, took a leading role in the project. The plan would evaluate the library's present condition and develop recommendations to guide its development for the next ten years. All aspects of the library's system would be included—collections, facilities, staffing, and technology.

A Microsoft volunteer teaches a class in the new Gates Training Center at the Central Library.

To begin the process, The Hillier Group coordinated a citywide survey during the summer of 1998 to gauge public opinion about the library and find out what citizens wanted. Among the chief complaints were outdated or inadequate materials, too few staff members, and inconvenient hours. The most common reasons for using the library (depending on the patron's age) were story times, pleasure reading, school assignments, financial planning, genealogy, curriculum support, professional research, and career guidance. Recommendations included sprucing up the facilities, extending the hours of service, adding more programs for young adults, and improving computer catalog and database training.[24] In 1999, the information gathering accelerated and library users were invited to participate in a series of twenty-eight public forums, at which they were asked to describe their ideal library. Interviews with community leaders and written surveys were also collected.[25]

A welcoming atmosphere was becoming increasingly important. Participants in the forums mentioned the coffee bars and comfortable chairs and couches now common in large bookstores, and they expressed a wish for those sorts of amenities in the library. "I think it's pretty consistent," library director Salazar said. "They want the library to sort of emulate Borders and other bookstores." Many of the comments from the previous year's survey were repeated: more parking, more computer terminals, reduced fines for overdue books.[26]

With this data in hand, The Hillier Group began researching population trends and conducting market studies with an eye toward identifying sites for future branch libraries. Their recommendations included replacing eight older branches, renovating ten branches with expanded facilities at five of them, and adding five new branches in projected growth areas. In addition, the plan recommended two smaller "neighborhood library centers" that would offer a selection of popular materials. Proposals for the Central Library included positioning it as a destination experience in the central business district by presenting outstanding programs and exhibits and highlighting the availability of the library's unique and special collections. The master plan also endorsed the floor-by-floor renovation of the Central Library building, utilizing the public-private partnership model used for the first floor, and it recommended upgrades including additional high-speed elevators, a café, and a six-story atrium enclosing the balconies on the front of the building.[27]

Technology has become increasingly important in libraries, and the master plan advocated additional measures to keep the Dallas Public Library on the leading edge of technology. These included doubling the number of computers available, introducing smart cards, and enhanced modes of collection access.[28] The plan also recommended an extensive staff recruitment and training program and a targeted effort to replace outdated collection materials and upgrade the library's holdings in specific areas.

Meanwhile, the library continued to garner significant private support. In September 1998 the Eugene McDermott Foundation offered $500,000 to launch the renovation of the Central Library's eighth floor, which housed the History and Social Sciences Division, if the Friends of the Dallas Public Library could raise an equal amount. The Friends accepted the challenge, and the city added $1 million. The Friends were also successful in winning a grant from the 1999 Crystal Charity Ball to fund a Mobile Learning Center to serve children in low-income and inner-city neighborhoods. The Ball sponsors pledged $322,086, but the event was so successful, they were able to give $437,973 for the project. The forty-foot Mobile Learning Center carried books for all ages and computer workstations offering homework, learning drills, and research assistance with math, science, history, and reading. The Friends estimated that the mobile center, which went into operation in February 2000, would reach 35,000 children each year. The Friends' own annual fund-raiser was also enjoying unprecedented success. An "Evening with Kate and Jim Lehrer" in 1999 had been projected to net $30,000; instead, it brought in $73,000.[29]

The library also enjoyed a valuable ally in Mayor Ron Kirk, who in 1999, for the third year, sponsored the children's summer reading program. For more than fifty years the library, with valuable support from the Friends, had encouraged children to read by sponsoring summer reading clubs, offering rewards for the number of books read or, beginning about 1990, for the number of hours spent reading. As part of his support for what was christened "The Mayor's Summer Reading Program," Mayor Kirk recruited sponsors who provided books, admission passes, coupons, and drawings for computers and other incentives. Mayor Kirk's involvement raised the program's visibility and attractiveness, so that in 1999 nearly 20,000 children (pre-school through age eighteen) participated. In addition to a party in August to celebrate their achievements, each child received a book courtesy of the Friends.

In 2000 the Friends of the Dallas Public Library, Inc., celebrated its 50th anniversary.[30] For half a century the Friends had supported a wide range of library endeavors, including exhibitions, the purchase of fine books and manuscripts, preservation microfilming, the summer reading program, and scholarships for staff members to pursue Master of Library Science degrees and to attend workshops and conferences. Among its anniversary events were two special exhibitions. The first, "Spirit and Splendor: Art and Ideas in Sacred Books and Manuscripts," was drawn exclusively from volumes that had been gifts of the Friends to the library's Fine Books Collection. This exhibition explored the splendid artistic accomplishments and the power of the ideas that appeared in illuminated manuscripts, works with fine typography and decorative bindings, and contemporary artist-designed volumes from both the Christian and non-Christian traditions. The second exhibition, "Spirit and Splendor: Texas and the Path to Independence," showcased the Friends' 50th anniversary gift to the library, the *Declaration of Causes*, a rare strategic document in which Texans justified taking action against Mexico at the same time that they sought to give the Mexican government written notice of their concerns. Preceding the Texas Declaration of Independence by four months, the *Declaration of Causes* is a seminal document in the movement towards Texas' independence. The library's copy is one of only six known copies of the Spanish language version, and the only one owned by a public library.[31] Other Friends' 50th anniversary events included a "Wishbone Festival," with the PBS-character Wishbone cheering along programs, contests, and games at every branch library and in the children's center of the Jonsson library; cash gifts to every branch library and public service division of the Jonsson library for staff support; and a spring luncheon featuring Texan Larry L. King as the guest speaker.[32]

The Friends' 50th anniversary celebration served as something of a dress rehearsal for the even bigger celebration of the library's 100th birthday in 2001. "Centennial Fest," the kick-off event on April 21-22, included a two-day street festival with music and entertainment, the annual book sale (this year with more than 125,000 books), children's programs and literary events—all designed to promote library programs and services. Beginning the week following Centennial Fest and continuing through the end of October, the twenty-two branches and Library-on-Wheels each held its own birthday celebration. A traveling exhibit with a historic photo/timeline of events in Dallas and the library over the past one hundred years visited each branch as part of its celebration. The library honored Dallas citizens who created and contributed to its century of success at a "Civic Salute Luncheon," while, for the first time, Texas Woman's University moved its Lillian Bradshaw Lecture to

Mayor Ron Kirk and Library Director Ramiro Salazar pose outside the Library on Wheels, a mobile learning unit funded by the Crystal Charity Ball in 1998.

Dallas. The Friends of the Dallas Public Library presented an arts series in cooperation with other local cultural institutions, showcasing music, dance, theater, and the visual arts. And the Friends dedicated their fall fundraising gala, comprising a banquet, silent auction, and author lecture, to the one hundredth birthday celebration.

As the Dallas Public Library concluded its first hundred years of service to the community, its future looked brighter than anyone could have predicted just a few years earlier.

Chapter 14

The Dallas Public Library: Today . . . and Tomorrow

In the hundred years from 1901 to 2001, Dallas grew from nine square miles to 385. Its population increased from 42,638 to more than 1 million. Dallas had become what civic leaders at the beginning of the twentieth century had hoped—one of the ten largest cities in the nation, the transportation center of its region and the financial capital of the Southwest.

During those same hundred years, the Dallas Public Library grew along with the city it served. When Andrew Carnegie made his initial gift to construct a library building, he required that the city pledge to contribute $4,000 a year toward its operation and upkeep. A century later, the library's annual operating budget tops $22 million.[1] The first librarian, Rosa Leeper, ran the library with a staff of five (including the janitor and a young man who helped out on weekends). Today the library employs some 569 individuals, 130 professional librarians and information specialists, along with library associates, customer service representatives, pages, and other support staff. Reflecting the wide public support that the Dallas library has always enjoyed, it also receives about 40,000 hours each year in volunteer service. And, of course, from a single downtown library, the Dallas system has expanded to comprise twenty-two branch libraries as well as a central library.[2]

In 1901, when the Dallas Public Library opened, 9,852 books were on the shelves. Today catalogued items total more than 2.5 million, and these include materials such as videotapes and compact disks not dreamed of a hundred years ago. Besides English, only a few foreign languages were represented in the original collection. Today, reflecting the diversity of the city's modern population, the Dallas Public Library carries materials in dozens of languages from every continent. Miss Leeper was justifiably proud that within ten weeks of the library's opening, 3,000 people had obtained borrower's cards. Today the number of cardholders is well over 500,000. These patrons checked out nearly 4 million items in 2000.

Yet circulation figures alone reflect only one aspect of the Dallas Public Library's use by the community. Many of the 2.5 million people who visited the Central Library or one of the branches during 2000 never checked out a book or a tape. During the year, the library system hosted nearly 9,000 programs. Both at the Central Library and the branches, children could attend "Toddler Time" or "Preschool Story Time," at which they might hear a story, watch a film, see a puppet show, or participate in age-specific activities. Older students could learn how to develop a successful Science Fair Project, discover the mysteries of the rainforest while creating a melodious rain stick, or learn about an ethnic holiday, such as Chinese New Year. Adult patrons could take a class in personal computers, or in using the Internet. Immigrants could take English as a Second Language classes, while others prepared for the General Equivalency Diploma (G.E.D.). Several branch libraries sponsored book discussion groups, creative writing workshops, and poetry readings.[3] Both the central and branch libraries presented special exhibits, both traveling shows and ones designed in-house. And all the libraries provided meeting space for community groups.[4] And then there are all the people who used the library's resources without actually entering one of its physical sites. The number of "hits" on its Web site, through which computer users can access a wide variety of information, is huge, and "growing exponentially," according to one administrator.[5]

The richness of these offerings reflects the Dallas Public Library's continuing commitment to high quality public service, one of the hallmarks of its history. It also reflects the dedication of the staff. Current director Ramiro Salazar notes that he receives far more calls and notes complimenting library staff than complaints, which is rare in any public service industry.[6] Yet Salazar and his staff are hardly content to rest on past or current successes. They are well aware of the challenges facing the library as it enters its second century. Many of the branch libraries need upgrading. Aside from the usual wear and tear experienced by any such facility over a period of twenty or thirty years, the branches are performing services not anticipated when they were constructed, particularly in the field of computer technology. Some lack space for expansion or adequate parking and may need to be completely relocated. The Master Plan addresses these needs and should help the City Council allocate funds in future bond proposals.

But, as always, the library will need to marshal support throughout the community. Other projects will be vying for a place in the bond package and, in any case, city bond funds tend to be designated for "bricks and mortar" projects. New facilities are important, but the materials housed within them, and the programs that can be offered the public, are critical. The Master Plan also examines staffing, technology, and collections needs at the library, making it the most comprehensive study ever done of the institution. The Friends of the Dallas Public Library, Inc. has already agreed to join with the Municipal Library Board in creating a Citizens' Group to raise private dollars to match bond money, with the funds earmarked for collections development and technology.

The materials budget, which was $1.3 million in 1993, has increased to $3.5 million, supplemented by several special funds that have been established by generous donors. But the library

The circulation desk in 1901 was elegant but far less efficient than its twenty-first-century counterpart.

As part of the renovation of the ground floor, the circulation desk was moved to a more central site.

still has gaps in its collections dating from the "lean" years. Because publishers tend to keep new books in print for a relatively brief period of time, it is often difficult to fill these gaps later. To the argument that the Internet will replace the need for books, Director Salazar points to the continued growth of bookstores, which have evolved into popular gathering places. Taking a page from the success of Borders and Barnes & Noble, the Central Library plans to introduce a small café, where patrons can enjoy a cup of coffee and a pastry. But of course the library will need to keep pace with modern technology. While the computer won't replace books—"at least for the foreseeable future!" admits Salazar—it does allow library users to access information more efficiently. The way the library does business will change. Library personnel will need to be more proficient in technology, to help users navigate through the many options. As a result, the Dallas Library will be placing increased emphasis on staff training and development.[7]

The library will continue to focus on services most important to its users. This may mean some re-allocation of resources. One goal, for instance, is to expand the hours of the branch libraries to six days a week.[8] Currently five of the branches are open on Sunday afternoons (in addition to five days during the rest of the week), and they experience some of their busiest times on Sundays. The Central Library, which is open seven days a week, is always busy. But its role, too, is changing. It remains a destination for genealogists, scholarly researchers, small business owners, and school groups. But with the recent increase in residents in and near the Central Business District, it is also filling the role of a "downtown branch." The Master Plan offers some suggestions on how to enhance the visibility of the Central Library, which the planners feel can be a major attraction downtown for visitors to the city. The Dallas Library has many assets that deserve to be better known. Its collection of rare and fine books, to cite one example, is outstanding. Salazar hopes to make these treasures of human knowledge more accessible, through exhib-

Mayor Ron Kirk welcomes a participant in the Mayor's Summer Reading Program at the library.

its, lectures, perhaps a special rare book room where patrons can see and experience them more easily.[9]

If visitors to the Central Library take the elevator to the eighth floor, they will encounter one of the largest and most comprehensive genealogy collections in the southern half of the nation. Researchers descend on this section daily to utilize 80,000 volumes, 42,000 rolls of microfilm, 77,000 sheets of microfiche, 1,200 microcards, and over 700 maps and charts. And genealogy represents only part of the History & Social Sciences Division that fills the entire floor, offering resources for learning more about both the United States and foreign countries with law books, education materials, and travel guides that run the gamut from Alaska to Zimbabwe. On special exhibit on this floor are items from the McDermott Collection of Navajo Blankets. One of the largest collections of Navajo wearing blankets on display in the world, the blankets are a gift from the Eugene McDermott Foundation. The blankets date from 1860 to 1918 and include a variety of weaving styles and techniques. The Eugene McDermott Foundation has given $1 million to underwrite the renovation of the eighth floor in honor of McDermott's love for history.

The library's Special Collections are housed on the seventh floor. Both the Texas/Dallas History & Archives Division and Fine Books hold some of the Dallas Public Library's most treasured items. Among these are a rare broadside copy of the *Declaration of Independence,* a gift to the city from a group of civic-minded citizens, and a Shakespeare First Folio, the gift of the Dallas Shakespeare Club in honor of its 100th anniversary. The *Declaration of Independence* is a rare treasure, indeed. Printed on the night of July 4, 1776, the broadside is one of twenty-five known to exist and the only copy housed in a public library. It is sometimes called the "Lost Copy" because it was found in storage in Leary's Book Store in Philadelphia in 1968 when that establishment closed after 132 years in business. Both of these precious artifacts are permanently displayed in specially designed exhibit areas.

The Fine Books collection focuses on the history of the book and the history of ideas. Many of the volumes are gifts of the Friends of the Dallas Public Library, Inc., or members of the Friends who have a special interest in fine printing and rare books. Among its treasures are a leaf from the Gutenberg Bible, a Babylonian clay tablet dating to 2095 B.C., Galileo's *Dialogo* of 1632, and a complete set of Denis Diderot's landmark *Encyclopedie*. The seventh floor's Virginia Lazenby O'Hara Gallery hosts rotating special exhibits drawn from library collections as well as traveling shows.

The Texas/Dallas History & Archives Division has one of the library's most important collections, focusing specifically on Dallas and the State of Texas. Newspapers, maps, manuscript collections, oral histories, city directories, yearbooks, and an extensive photograph collection supplement a core collection of often-rare historical books. Because Texas/Dallas is also a depository for the state's Regional Historical Resource Depository (RHRD) program, it includes many Dallas County records, including civil district court records from 1846 to 1939. As keeper of the Dallas Public Library's own history, it even retains and uses sturdy tables from the old Carnegie Library.

In 1999 patrons were invited to participate in an "Express Yourself" poetry contest.

The sixth floor houses the Government Information Center. Because the library has been a U. S. Federal Depository since 1902, the collection includes a complete set of the American State Papers, U. S. Serial Set, and major federal finding aids, as well as consumer information, business statistics, census and weather data, income tax forms and publications, Congressional hearings, bills, and reports, and NASA documents. The Center also includes publications issued by the City of Dallas, the State of Texas, and international organizations such as the United Nations, as well as an extensive map and atlas collection. An area that enjoys especially heavy use is the patents, trademarks, and copyrights collection. Patrons can conduct a preliminary patent or trademark search, pick up a copyright application form, or take a look at "how to" books on patents, copyright, trade secrets, and trademarks.

A newly remodeled, state-of-the-art Business and Technology Center opened on the fifth floor in December 1998. Funded by a $1 million gift from Mrs. Nancy Hamon in honor of her late husband, Jake L. Hamon, the project established the Jake and Nancy Hamon Oil and Gas Resource Center, where patrons can search a myriad of electronic databases related to the petroleum industry. Researchers can also find information on business history, industry statistics, corporate finances, tax law, marketing research aids, and most other areas of business concern in a comfortable, well-lit, state-of-the-art facility.

The Fine Arts Division occupies the fourth floor. In addition to an extensive collection of books and periodicals on art, music, dance, theater, film, fashion, and architecture, this division also holds significant manuscript collections relating to the performing and visual arts in Dallas. Gallery 4 features rotating displays by new and emerging local artists. The upcoming fourth floor renovation will be underwritten by a $1 million grant from the Hoblitzelle Foundation.

The Humanities Division on the third floor contains the library's fiction collection, as well as extensive resources for the study of literature, religion, and the humanities. Writers working on extended projects at the library may apply to use the Frances Sanger

Mossiker Writers Study Room on this floor. Named for the noted Dallas author, this room offers writers a place to store the research materials they are using and to work more closely with the library's professional staff. Along with the Children's Center on the second floor, the Humanities Division is one of the most heavily patronized areas in the Central Library.

The award-winning Children's Center opened in 1989. Completely funded by benefactors, the floor features specially designed areas for storytelling, puppet and film shows, and exhibits. In addition to the wide range of books, magazines, books-on-tape, and videos available for checkout, the Children's Center also holds the Siddie Joe Johnson Children's Literature Collection, a collection unique in the Southwest. Named for the beloved former children's librarian, the collection contains some 4,000 books, including 109 editions of Mother Goose, 200 volumes of fairy tales, 545 first editions, and early texts, primers, and religious tracts for children.

The recent renovation of the ground floor moved library materials and circulation functions to the foreground and established Library Online, with banks of Internet and Internet/office application computers.[10] This extremely popular service complements the more traditional functions of the General Reference/Current Collection Division housed nearby. Designed to function as a combination branch library ambiance of a bookstore, the division offers telephone reference and a popular reading collection of best sellers as well as books-on-tape and CD, videos, large-print books, and

"Wishbone," the protagonist of PBS's popular children's program, joins Carol Dumont in celebrating the fiftieth anniversary of the Friends of the Dallas Public Library, Inc., in 2000.

Constructed in 1903 just a few blocks from the Carnegie Library, the Wilson Building is one of the architectural jewels of Dallas. In 1999 it was converted into luxury loft apartments, reflecting an upsurge in downtown living. The thousands of residents now living in the Wilson and other historic buildings, as well as in new apartments constructed in the downtown area, are within walking distance of the Central Library, which functions, in effect, as their "branch library."

materials geared to appeal to teenage readers.

The guiding philosophy of the Dallas Public Library has always been service to its patrons. Adapting to the changing nature of those patrons is a continuing challenge. The new immigrant groups from Asia, Africa, the Middle East, and Central and South America who make up an increasing proportion of Dallas's population bring with them varied cultures, languages, and educational backgrounds, each with subtle but distinct differences. This population is often unaware of the services the library can offer them, but the library is determined to reach out to these newcomers and try to meet their needs. A mobile unit—descendant of the old bookmobiles—that offers special after-school programs to immigrant and minority children is one tool currently being tried. Emerging technology may offer other tools.[11]

The Dallas Public Library continues to be fortunate in the support it enjoys. The Municipal Library Advisory Board, whose members are appointed by the City Council, serves as an advocate of the library with the Council and in other forums. Reflecting as they do the diversity of the city, the board members also provide the library director with important advice on the community's needs. The Friends of the Dallas Public Library continues to live up to its reputation as the best public library friends' group in the country. The Friends have recently pledged to raise $3 million to match a $1 million challenge grant from Margaret McDermott. With the support of Mayor Ron Kirk and City Manager Ted Benavides, the city has committed to match this $4 million total. Thus the public/private partnership that built the Central Library is working again to restore and position the building for the twenty-first century. The funds raised will be used to renovate the remaining floors of the Central Library, following similar successful projects that refurbished the first, second, fifth, and eighth floors. Among the hallmarks of these renovations have been making more of the collection accessible to the public, improving lighting, upgrading computers and making more of them available, and giving each floor a distinctive ambience appropriate for its collections.

Given this combination of a valuable product and strong support, it's not surprising that Director Ramiro Salazar says, "I see a bright future for the Dallas Public Library."[12] Assistant Director Joe Bearden agrees, expressing the hope that the Centennial Celebration will provide an opportunity to reinvigorate the broad-based community commitment to the public library that characterized Dallas clubwomen, businessmen, schoolteachers and children a hundred years ago.[13] Lillian Bradshaw, whose association with the Dallas Public Library covers more than half its history, endorses this vision. "I want to see the Dallas Public Library be a library for all the citizens of Dallas, regardless of ethnicity," she observes. "It has the potential to do this, but it must continue to gather support from the entire community."[14] If this happens, the efforts of May Exall and the other founders will be justified, and the Dallas Public Library will continue to be a crown jewel of the city for centuries to come.

If Mrs. Exall and the other founders of the Dallas Public Library could gaze into the institution's future via the computer, what might they see?

Appendix

Directors of the Dallas Public Library*

Rosa Leeper	1900–1916
Betsy Wiley	1916–1922
Cleora Clanton	1922–1954
James Meeks	1955–1961
Lillian Moore Bradshaw	1961–1984
Patrick O'Brien	1984–1992
Ramiro Salazar	1993–present

* Rosa Leeper, Betsy Wiley, and Cleora Clanton held the official position of "Librarian." Beginning with James Meeks, the title was "Director."

Presidents of the Board of Trustees of the Dallas Public Library

May Dickson Exall	1901–1910
Maurice E. Locke	1910–1919
Edward A. Belsterling	1919–1925
W. T. Henry	1925–1932
Edward A. Belsterling	1932–1944
Hugo Schoellkopf	1944–1945
Alfonso Johnson	1945–1948
Boude Storey	1949–1958
Roscoe L. Thomas	1958–1961
Hawkins Menefee	1963–1966
Dr. Arthur A. Smith	1966–1973

Chairs of the Municipal Library Advisory Board

Mrs. Adelfa B. Callejo	1973–1975
Jerry L. Fitzgerald	1975–1979
Charlotte Geary	1979–1985
Linda Hankinson	1985- 1989
Marguerite S. Foster	1989–1991
Eloise R. Sherman	1991–1994
Lee Simpson	1994–present

Notes

Chapter One: Building a Library

1. Maxine Holmes and Gerald D. Saxon, eds., *The WPA Dallas Guide and History* (n.p.: Dallas Public Library, Texas Center for the Book, University of North Texas Press, 1992), 359.

2. "The Pierian Family," unpublished manuscript in Pierian Collection, Dallas Historical Society; *The Dallas Morning News*, March 12, 1999.

3. Jackie McElhaney, "Dallas Public Schools: The First Decade," *Heritage News* 9, no. 1 (Spring 1984): 14.

4. *The Dallas Morning News*, November 29, 1897. For more on the remarkable Mrs. Miner and her work on behalf of public libraries, see Jacquelyn Masur McElhaney, *Pauline Periwinkle and Progressive Reform in Dallas* (College Station: Texas A & M University Press, 1997), 77–80.

5. *The Dallas Morning News*, October 27, 1898.

6. George S. Bobinski, *Carnegie Libraries* (Chicago: American Library Association, 1969), 9–13; Theodore Jones, *Carnegie Libraries Across America: A Public Legacy* (New York: Preservation Press, 1997), 1–13.

7. *The Dallas Times Herald*, September 29, 1936.

8. *History of the Dallas Federation of Women's Clubs, 1898–1936* (Dallas: n.d.), 15–16.

9. *The Dallas Morning News*, March 7, 1899.

10. Ibid., March 12, 1899.

11. Ibid., March 31, 1899.

12. Ibid., May 11, 1899.

13. Minutes, Dallas Library Association Board of Trustees, April 26, 1899, Dallas Public Library Archives.

14. *The Dallas Morning News,* May 10, 1899.

15. Ibid., April 4, 1899.

16. Ibid., April 10, 1899.

17. May D. Exall, "The First Year of the City Federation of Women's Clubs and the First Work Undertaken by the Federation—The Founding of a Free Public Library in Dallas," typescript in Dallas Public Library Archives.

18. Mrs. Henry Exall to Andrew Carnegie, August 7, 1899, Carnegie Corporation Archives.

19. May D. Exall, "The First Year."

20. Andrew Carnegie to Mrs. Henry Exall, August 23, 1899, published in *Dallas Times Herald*, September 19, 1899.

21. *Dallas Times Herald,* September 19, 1899.

22. May D. Exall, "The First Year"; Minutes, DLA Board of Trustees, March 6, 1900.

23. May D. Exall, "The First Year."

24. Ibid.

25. Report by John Lawrence Mauran, July 19, 1900, Minutes of DPL Board of Trustees; letter of John Lawrence Mauran to Joseph Dickson, July 20, 1900, DPL Archives.

26. Minutes of DPL Board of Trustees, October 10, 1900; *The Dallas Morning News*, January 17, 1901; May D. Exall, "The First Year."

27. Remarks at grand opening of library, *Dallas Times Herald*, October 30, 1901.

28. Minutes of DPL Board of Trustees, February 26, 1901; DPL records.

29. Ibid., July 1, 1901.

30. May D. Exall, "The First Year."

31. *The Dallas Morning News*, October 30, 1901.

32. *Dallas Times Herald*, October 30, 1901.

Chapter Two: Growing Pains

1. Rosa M. Leeper, "The Dallas (Texas) Public Library," *The Library Journal* (February 1902): 79; reports of Rosa Leeper to the Board of Trustees, February 13 and March 13, 1902, Dallas Public Library Archives.

2. Leeper, "Dallas Public Library," 79.

3. Miss Leeper reported the Reverchon gift to the Trustees in March 1903. Many of the Reverchon and Green books remain in the library's collection, complete with the bookplates of their donors.

4. May D. Exall, "The First Year of the City Federation of Women's Clubs and the First Work Undertaken by the Federation—The Founding of a Free Public Library in Dallas," typescript in the Dallas Public Library Archives.

5. Report of Rosa Leeper to the Trustees, October 1903.

6. Ibid., February 1903.

7. Ibid., May 1903.

8. Ibid., November 1903.

9. Leeper, "Dallas Public Library."

10. Rosa M. Leeper, *Dallas Public Library Annual Report for the Year Ending April 30, 1908*, 18.

11. Ibid., 19–20.

12. Larry Grove, *The Dallas Public Library: The First 75 Years* (Dallas: Dallas Public Library, 1977), 41.

13. Mrs. Henry Exall to Andrew Carnegie, May 3 and December 4, 1904; James Bertram to Mrs. Exall, December 11, 1907, Carnegie Corporation Archives.

14. *The Dallas Morning News*, November 1, 1901.

15. Exall, "The First Year."

16. Geraldine P. Cristol, "The History of the Dallas Museum of Fine Arts" (M.A. Thesis, SMU, 1970), 18.

17. Michael V. Hazel, "Art for the People: Dallas' First Public Gallery," *Heritage News*, 9, no. 3 (Fall 1984): 4–8.

18. Leeper, *Annual Report for 1908*, 19.

19. Exall, "The First Year."

20. Dallas Public Library Annual Report, 1916–17.

21. Exall, "The First Year."

22. Minutes, DPL Board of Trustees, January 13 and February 10, 1910.

23. Ibid., June 8, 1916.

24. Ibid., May 10, 1917.

25. DPL Annual Report, 1916–17.

26. Ibid., 1917–18.
27. Ibid.
28. Ibid.
29. Minutes, DPL Board of Trustees, June 30, 1920.
30. DPL Annual Report, 1919–20.
31. DPL Annual Report, 1921–22.
32. Minutes, DPL Board of Trustees, May 13, 1920, and October 1922.
33. *Dallas Times Herald*, November 11, 1954.

Chapter Three: Branching Out

1. Bill Minutgalio and Holly Williams, *The Hidden City: Oak Cliff, Texas* (Elmwood Press and The Old Oak Cliff Conservation League, 1990), 52–89.

2. Minutes, Board of Trustees Meeting, June 13, 1903. The original "Rules and Regulations" for the Dallas Public Library, approved in July 1901, had stated that "all white persons . . . who reside within three and a half miles of the Dallas postoffice" could withdraw books. The three-and-a-half mile limit was adequate for the original township of Oak Cliff, but by 1910, as the entire city expanded, the board amended the rules to read "ten miles." See copy in Dallas Public Library Archives.

3. Ibid., April 18, 1911.

4. Ruth Sibley, "Oak Cliff Library Is Oldest Branch in Dallas," *The Oak Cliff Tribune*, June 25, 1953.

5. James Richard Beaupre, "The Founding and Development of the Jefferson Branch Library," unpublished paper, April 21, 1961, in Dallas Public Library Archives.

6. James Bertram to Maurice Locke, June 24, 1911, Carnegie Corporation archives.

7. Heidi Gale Stein, "Dallas Public Library's Association with Andrew Carnegie's Library Philanthropy," unpublished paper, 1987, in Dallas Public Library archives.

8. *The Dallas Morning News*, September 8, 12, and 14, 1911.

9. Kathy Toon, "A Brief History of the Oak Cliff Branch of the Dallas Public Library," unpublished paper, North Texas State University, May 7, 1975.

10. James Bertram to Maurice Locke, December 23, 1913, Carnegie Foundation Archives.

11. Maurice Locke to James Bertram, December 29, 1913, Carnegie Foundation Archives.

12. *The Dallas Morning News*, March 17, 1914.

13. Dallas Public Library Annual Report, 1915–16.

14. Cary Sue White, "Cliff Branch Library Started in April 1914," *Dallas Dispatch Journal* (Oak Cliff Edition), July 13, 1939.

15. DPL Annual Report, 1916–17.

16. Ibid., 1925–26.

17. Sibley, "Oak Cliff Branch."

18. DPL Annual Report, 1917–18.

19. Ibid., 1937.

20. *The Dallas Morning News*, July 24, 1952.

21. Minutes, Board of Trustees meetings, October, November, and December 1927, and January, February, and April 1928.

22. DPL Annual Report, 1950–51.

23. *Oak Cliff Tribune*, September 28, 1950; *The Dallas Morning News*, August 29, 1957; *The Dallas Morning News*, January 23, 1958.

24. Lowell A. Martin, "Branch Library Services for Dallas," (1958), 35–6, Dallas Public Library Archives.

25. Toon, "A Brief History of the Oak Cliff Branch."

Chapter Four: The Dunbar Branch

1. Mrs. Henry Exall to Andrew Carnegie, August 7, 1899, Carnegie Corporation Archives.

2. Jacquelyn M. McElhaney, "Childhood in Dallas, 1870–1900" (M.A. Thesis, Southern Methodist University, 1982), 28–31.

3. Minutes of Board of Trustees meeting, July 1, 1901; printed copy of "Rules and Regulations, Dallas Public Library," DPL Archives.

4. Letter to Mrs. R. T. Hamilton and Mrs. M. C. Cooper, July 17, 1906, signed by A. V. Lane, Joseph M. Dickson, and J. T. Howard, included in Minutes of Board of Trustees meeting, October 3, 1906.

5. Letter from The Colored Library Association to the President and Board of Trustees of the Dallas Public Library Association, June 26, 1907, Carnegie Corporation Archives. The signatories include such prominent citizens as Doc Rowan, a merchant; N. W. Harllee, principal of the Colored High School; B. F. Darrell, principal of the Ninth Ward Public School; Dr. M. C. Cooper, a dentist; and several ministers.

6. Minutes of Board of Trustees meeting, January 9, 1908.

7. Letter from The Colored Library Association to Andrew Carnegie, February 10, 1909, Carnegie Corporation Archives.

8. Letter from James Bertram (Carnegie's secretary) to M. C. Cooper, President, Dallas Colored Library Association, April 29, 1909, Carnegie Corporation Archives.

9. Joseph E. Wiley to James Bertram, November 28, 1911, and James Bertram to Joseph E. Wiley, December 19, 1911, Carnegie Corporation Archives.

10. M. M. Rodgers to James Bertram, December 4, 1915, Carnegie Corporation Archives.

11. Sam Acheson, *Dallas Yesterday* (Dallas: SMU Press, 1977), 175.

12. Henry D. Lindsley to James Bertram, January 8, 1916, Carnegie Corporation Archives.

13. James Bertram to Will C. McGintie, secretary to the mayor, February 8, 1916, Carnegie Corporation Archives.

14. Henry D. Lindsley to James Bertram, April 24, 1916, Carnegie Corporation Archives.

15. James Bertram to Henry D. Lindsley, June 6, 1916, Carnegie Corporation Archives.

16. Henry D. Lindsley to James Bertram, June 27, 1916, Carnegie Corporation Archives.

17. James Bertram to Henry D. Lindsley, July 1, 1916, and Henry D. Lindsley to James Bertram, July 11, 1916, Carnegie Corporation Archives.

18. "Carnegie Libraries," in *American Greats*, edited by Robert A. Wilson and Stanley Marcus (New York: Public Affairs, 1999), 38–9.

19. Minutes of Board of Trustees meeting, December 12, 1912. Mrs. Isadore Miner married W. A. Callaway in 1900 and continued to use the Pauline Periwinkle penname.

20. See Minutes of Board of Trustees, January 13, 1910, January 13, 1916, and January 13, 1921.

21. Darwin Payne, "*The Dallas Morning News* and the Ku Klux Klan," *Legacies* 9, no. 1 (Spring 1997): 16–27.

22. Robert B. Fairbanks, *For the City as a Whole: Planning, Politics, and the Public Interest in Dallas, Texas 1900–1965* (Columbus: Ohio State University Press, 1998), 53.

23. Dallas Public Library Annual Report, 1925–26.

24. T. D. Marshall, Chairman, Colored Teachers' State Association of Texas, to Dallas Public Library Board, March 8, 1929; C. M. Moore, Business Manager, Dallas Public Schools, to Edward W. Belsterling, June 14, 1929; both in DPL Archives, "Dunbar Branch" folder.

25. See Minutes of Board of Trustees, June 28, 1928, April 29, 1929, February 1930, and November 3, 1930.

26. *Dallas Express*, June 17, 1931.

27. Cleora Clanton to Earl Goforth, City Secretary, May 7, 1931, and list of books; both in DPL Archives, "Dunbar Branch" folder.

28. *Dallas Express*, July 25, 1936.

29. John William Rogers, "Valuable Service Rendered by Public Library," *Dallas Times Herald*, August 8, 1937.

30. *Dallas Express*, October 15, 1938.

31. Ibid., August 26, 1939.

32. Ibid., May 18, 1940.

33. De Artis Pryor, chairman, Delta Library Committee, to Edward Belsterling, President of the Dallas Library Board, April 15, 1940; Cleora Clanton to Miss De Artis Pryor, June 15, 1940; and De Artis Pryor to Cleora Clanton, July 2, 1940; all in DPL Archives, "Dunbar Branch" folder.

34. *Dallas Star Post*, November 21, 1953.

35. Interview with Lillian Bradshaw, January 17, 2001. Mrs. Bradshaw recalled that black patrons were seated in an area at the back of the Carnegie Library and materials were brought to them. Her memory was confirmed by Tom Bogie, who witnessed such an occasion while he worked in the reference department in 1952. Interview with Tom Bogie, January 29, 2001.

36. Lowell Martin, "Survey of Branch Libraries," January 1958, DPL Archives.

37. *The Dallas Morning News*, May 15, 1959.

38. The city attempted unsuccessfully to sell the Dunbar building in 1959. Several small church groups rented the building during the next few years, but by 1966 it was empty and had been vandalized. In 1967 it was sold for $8,500 to St. John's Baptist Church, which was located on the same block. See memoranda in DPL Archives, "Dunbar Branch" file.

Chapter Five: The Clanton Administration

1. *Dallas Times Herald*, undated clipping in scrapbook at Dallas Public Library. Although the clipping is undated, the context would seem to place it about 1923 or 1924.

2. Dallas Public Library Annual Report, 1925–26.

3. Larry Grove, *The Dallas Public Library: The First 75 Years* (Dallas: Dallas Public Library, 1977), 51.

4. Ibid., 50.

5. *Dallas Dispatch*, March 2, 1926.

6. Ibid., March 4, 1926.

7. DPL Annual Report, 1923–24.

8. Unidentified clipping, c. 1922, in scrapbook "1921–1942" at Dallas Public Library.

9. DPL Annual Report, 1925–26.

10. *Dallas Times Herald*, October 24, 1926.

11. DPL Annual Report, 1924–25.

12. Ibid., 1925–26.

13. *The Dallas Morning News*, January 21, 25, and 30, 1927. See also Minutes of the Board of Trustees, January 29, 1927.

14. DPL Annual Report, 1927–28.

15. Minutes of DPL Board of Trustees, June 28, 1928; September 28, 1928; May 29, 1929; and February 1930.

16. Ibid., December 11, 1930.

17. Grove, *The First 75 Years*, 55.

18. DPL Annual Reports, 1929–30 and 1930–31.

19. Interview with Marion Underwood, April 24, 1973, in Gerald D. Saxon, ed., *Reminiscences: A Glimpse of Old East Dallas* (Dallas: Dallas Public Library, 1983), 94–101.

20. DPL Annual Report, 1934.

21. *Dallas Times Herald*, November 3, 1933.

22. Job descriptions prepared by Cleora Clanton, and letter from Grace E. Williams, Supervisor of Women's Work, Works Progress Administration, to Cleora Clanton, November 21, 1935.

23. DPL Annual Report, 1936.

24. Ibid., 1939.

25. *Dallas Times Herald*, November 12, 1936.

26. DPL Annual Report, 1936.

27. Cleora Clanton to John William Rogers, July 23, 1937; John William Rogers, "Valuable Service Rendered Dallas by Public Library," *Dallas Times Herald*, August 8, 1937.

28. DPL Annual Reports, 1934 and 1935, among others.

29. *Dallas Times Herald*, April 7, 1938.

30. *The Dallas Morning News*, July 30, 1941.

31. Ibid., September 4, 1941.

32. Ibid., September 5, 1941.

33. DPL Annual Report, 1940–41.

34. Ibid., 1942–43. A library pamphlet, "This Is Our War . . . Let's Read About It," described the Dallas Public Library's resources in some detail; DPL Archives, "1940–49 History" file.

35. For examples of programs, see scrapbook in Dallas Public Library Archives covering children's activities from 1928 to 1939.

36. *The Dallas Morning News*, August 8, 1965.

37. *Dallas Times Herald*, June 24, 1954.

38. Interview with Tom Bogie, January 29, 2001.

39. *Dallas Times Herald*, May 24, 1945.

40. *The Dallas Morning News*, January 4, 1948.

41. Ibid., February 10 and 12, 1948.

42. Ibid., March 4, 1948.

43. DPL Annual Reports, 1939 and 1940.

44. See Mrs. Bradshaw's reports, addenda to the DPL Annual Reports 1947—1951.

45. *Dallas Times Herald*, November 27, 1949.

46. *The Dallas Morning News*, July 31, 1949, and August 3, 1949.

47. *Dallas Times Herald*, July 15, 1949, and November 6, 1949.

48. DPL Annual Report, 1950–52.

49. Ibid., 1947.

Chapter Six: Building a New Central Library

1. *The Dallas Morning News*, February 12, 1950.

2. Joseph W. McKnight, "Jones, Erin Bain," in *The New Handbook of Texas* (Austin: Texas State Historical Association, 1996).

3. Ruth Morgan, "Friends Win Campaign," *Library Journal* 79, no. 9 (May 1, 1954): 3.

4. *The Dallas Morning News*, November 1 and 5, 1950, and July 13, 1951.

5. Ibid., October 31, 1951.

6. *Dallas Times Herald*, July 13, 1951.

7. *The Dallas Morning News*, March 30, 1952.

8. *Dallas Times Herald*, April 30, 1952.

9. Joseph L. Wheeler and John Hall Jacobs, "Report of a Survey of the Public Library Situation at Dallas, Texas" (1952), 18–19.

10. *Dallas Times Herald*, May 7, 1952.

11. *The Dallas Morning News,* July 17, 1952.

12. Ibid., July 19, 1952.

13. Ibid., October 6, 1953. The Dallas Public Library scrapbooks for 1952 and 1953 contain numerous articles tracing this debate.

14. Wheeler and Jacobs, "Report," 36–37.

15. *Dallas Times Herald*, August 8, 1952.

16. David Dillon, *Dallas Architecture, 1936–1986* (Austin: Texas Monthly Press, 1985).

17. *Dallas Times Herald*, April 28, 1953.

18. Lillian Bradshaw, interview conducted by Gerald D. Saxon, August 17, 1998, p. 69.

19. *The Dallas Morning News*, January 12, 1954.

20. Interview with Byrdie Burras, January 10, 2001.

21. *Dallas Times Herald*, January 2, 1954.

22. *Dallas Times Herald*, January 27, 1954.

23. *The Dallas Morning News*, March 29, 1954 and April 4, 1954; *Dallas Times Herald*, March 29, 1954 and April 4, 1954.

24. *Dallas Times Herald*, March 11, 1954.

25. Morgan, "Friends Win Campaign," 7.

26. Interview with Lillian Bradshaw, January 17, 2001.

27. *Informer*, April 29, 1937.

28. *The Dallas Morning News*, February 25, 1953.

29. Ibid., February 24, 1952.

30. Bradshaw interview, August 17, 1998, p. 69; confirmed in interview, January 17, 2001.

31. *The Dallas Morning News*, November 17, 1954.

32. Ibid., November 11 and 17, 1954; *Dallas Times Herald*, November 18, 1954.

33. *The Dallas Morning News*, January 4, 1955.

34. Ibid., October 5, 1968.

35. Bradshaw interview January 17, 2001.

36. Bradshaw interview, August 17, 1998, p. 78.

37. Response by James Meeks to Denver University Library School Alumni Association newsletter, March 30, 1955, DPL Archives.

38. *Dallas Times Herald*, January 30 and March 29, 1955.

39. Ibid., May 8, 1955.

40. *The Dallas Morning News*, June 2, 1955.

41. Ibid., June 28, 1955.

42. Ibid., July 1, 1955.

43. Ibid., July 9, 1955.

44. Minutes, Board of Trustees, July 6 and July 20, 1955.

45. *The Dallas Morning News,* July 23, 26, and 28, 1955.

Chapter Seven: Settling In

1. *Dallas Times Herald*, September 6, 1955.

2. *The Dallas Morning News*, September 7, 1955.

3. *Dallas Times Herald*, September 16, 1955 and September 26, 1955; *The Dallas Morning News*, September 26, 1955.

4. Two letters in "History—1950s" file, DPL Archives. Meeks also read one of the letters to the Board of Trustees; see Minutes, December 15, 1955.

5. *The Dallas Morning News*, November 17, 1955.

6. *Dallas Times Herald*, May 16, 1956.

7. Lillian Moore Bradshaw, *Celebrating the First 50 Years: Friends of the Dallas Public Library, 1950–2000* (Dallas: Dallas Public Library, 2000), 12–13.

8. *The Dallas Morning News*, January 25, 1956, and September 30, 1956.

9. Ibid., August 2, 1956.

10. Interview with Lillian Bradshaw, August 17, 1998, pp.88–89.

11. When the new Central Library opened in 1982, the sculpture was left behind. In 1993 it was sold by the Federal Deposit Insurance Corp. (which by then owned the Commerce Street building) to a Saginaw, Michigan, gallery that housed a large collection of works by Fredericks. The city of Dallas had declined to buy it for $20,000, saying it couldn't afford the maintenance costs. *The Dallas Morning News*, April 7, 1993.

12. Affidavit by James Meeks, August 1957, DPL Archives.

13. *Dallas Times Herald*, November 21, 1956.

14. Darwin Payne, *Big D: Triumphs and Troubles of an American Supercity in the 20th Century* (Dallas: Three Forks Press, 2000), 327–8.

15. Minutes, Board of Trustees, November 21, 1956; *The Dallas Morning News*, November 22, 1956.

16. Adrian A. Paradia, "Librarians Wanted: Careers in Library Service" (New York: David McKay Company, 1959), photocopied excerpt in DPL Archives.

17. *The Dallas Morning News*, July 6, 1955, and August 17, 1957.

18. Interview with Tom Bogie, January 30, 2001.

19. Copies from various newspapers, July 28, 1957, in DPL scrapbook.

20. *The Dallas Morning* News, August 14, 1957.

21. Articles from various newspapers, from Massachusetts to California, December 1957, in DPL scrapbook.

22. Stanley Marcus, *Minding the Store* (Denton: University of North Texas Press, facsimile edition, 1997), 210.

23. *Dallas Times Herald*, October 13, 1958.

24. *The Dallas Morning News*, February 7, 1958.

25. Ibid., December 4, 1960.

26. *Dallas Times Herald*, January 8 and 31, 1965.

27. *The Dallas Morning News*, August 24 and 27, 1958.

28. Ibid., September 14 and October 12, 1958; *Dallas Times Herald*, March 20 and April 12, 1958.

29. Minutes, Board of Trustees, April 10, 1957.

30. *Galveston Daily News*, January 5, 1958; *Waco Herald*, August 12, 1958; *Dallas Times Herald*, April 9, 1959; Memo from Meeks to Board of Trustees, April 8, 1959.

31. *The Dallas Morning News*, October 2, 1960.

32. Undated report in DPL scrapbook.

Chapter Eight: Branching Out All Over

1. In an interview in 1964, Cleora Clanton revealed that the library board had objected to the Sanger site from the beginning. "We were railroaded into it," she said, "and knew it shouldn't be located there." "We got no help from the city administration and the location was against our consciences," she continued. "The present library staff shouldn't be blamed for the lack of use. It was a bad location from the very start." *(Dallas Times Herald*, April 22, 1964.)

2. Interview with Marion Underwood, April 24, 1973, in Gerald D. Saxon, ed., *Reminiscences: A Glimpse of Old East Dallas* (Dallas: Dallas Public Library, 1983), 97, 99.

3. *Walnut Hill Journal*, July 26, 1956, and October 25, 1956.

4. *Dallas Times Herald*, May 20, 1957.

5. *The Dallas Morning News*, May 29, 1957; *Dallas Times Herald*, June 13, 1957.

6. Lowell A. Martin, "Library Services for Dallas" (1958), 5–6.

7. Ibid., 64–65.

8. Ibid., 65.

9. Ibid., 41–42.

10. Summary report by Sam G. Whitton, in DPL scrapbook.

11. *The Dallas Morning News*, December 3, 1958.

12. Ibid., June 3, 1959, July 28, 1959; *Dallas Times Herald*, August 4, 1959; November 23, 1960; August 3, 1961; Wyman Jones, "Dallas Draws a Double," *Library Journal* (December 1, 1962), 4365.

13. *Dallas Times Herald*, December 10 and 11, 1959.

14. Ibid., November 30, 1960; Jones, "Dallas Draws a Double," 4365.

15. *The Dallas Morning News*, January 7, 1962.

16. Jones, "Dallas Draws a Double," 4364–65.

17. *The Dallas Morning News*, December 16, 1959, December 16, 1960, December 21, 1960, and February 9, 1961; *Dallas Times Herald*, December 6 and 14, 1960.

18. Martin, "Library Services," 42–3.

19. *Dallas Times Herald*, September 23, 1960.

20. *The Dallas Morning News*, February 1, 1959, and May 15, 1959. The Dunbar library building was leased in 1960 to the North Dallas Church of Christ; see Minutes, Board of Trustees, April 13, 1960.

21. *Dallas Times Herald*, May 6, 1965, and January 5, 1968.

22. Minutes, Board of Trustees, March 12, 1958.

23. *Dallas Times Herald*, April 4, 1962.

24. Ibid., August 8, 1962.

25. Jones, "Dallas Draws a Double," 4364.

Chapter Nine: The Bradshaw Years

1. *Dallas Times Herald*, August 18, 1961.

2. The Board of Trustees officially accepted Meeks's resignation on September 13, 1960, and directed that a letter be sent to him expressing its appreciation for his six and a half years of service; see Minutes, Board of Trustees.

3. Lillian Bradshaw interview, August 17, 1998, 92.

4. *Dallas Times Herald*, September 16, 1961.

5. Ibid., March 1, 1962. See also Minutes, Board of Trustees, February 28, 1961. Mrs. Bradshaw has credited oilman Jake Hamon with casting the deciding vote in her favor; interview with Lillian Bradshaw, January 17, 2001.

6. *Dallas Times Herald*, September 16, 1961.

7. Lillian Bradshaw, interview with Gerald Saxon, August 19, 1998, 206.

8. Ibid., 4.

9. Darwin Payne, *Big D: Triumphs and Troubles of an American Supercity in the 20th Century* (Dallas: Three Forks Press, 2000), 351.

10. Bradshaw interview, August 18, 1998, 93.

11. *Dallas Times Herald*, March 7, 1962.

12. Ibid., March 11, 1962.

13. Ibid.

14. Bradshaw interview, August 18, 1998, 95–96.

15. *The Dallas Morning News*, March 13, 1962.

16. *Dallas Times Herald*, March 15, 1962.

17. Minutes, Board of Trustees, March 14 and May 9, 1962; *The Dallas Morning News*, March 15 and May 10, 1962.

18. Bradshaw interview, January 17, 2001.

19. *The Dallas Morning News*, January 24, 1962.

20. Wyman Jones, "The Making of the Vote," *Library Journal* (March 1, 1962), 935, 951.

21. *Dallas Times Herald*, February 15, 1962.

22. Ibid., April 24, 1963.

23. Ibid., April 10, 1963.

24. Ibid., March 1, March 8, and May 14, 1964; Wyman Jones, "That Was the Day That Was," *Library Journal* (July 1964), 2752.

25. *The Dallas Morning News*, July 9, 1964 and February 5, 1965.

26. Interview with Linda Allmand, January 7, 2001.

27. *The Dallas Morning News*, March 7, 1965.

28. *Dallas Times Herald*, February 2, 1965.

29. *The Dallas Morning News*, March 9, 1965; *Dallas Times Herald*, April 15, 1965.

30. *The Dallas Morning News*, July 22, 1965.

31. Ibid., October 29, 1965.

32. Interview with David Henington, January 7, 2001.

33. *The Dallas Morning News*, March 30, 1967.

34. Bradshaw interview, August 19, 1998, 53.

35. *Dallas Times Herald*, November 18, 1963.

36. Lillian Moore Bradshaw, *Celebrating the First 50 Years: Friends of the Dallas Public Library, 1950–2000* (Dallas: Dallas Public Library, 2000), 14–16.

37. Ibid., 17.

38. *Dallas Times Herald*, August 26, 1966.

39. "A Decade of Service" (brochure, 1965).

Chapter Ten: Setting and Fulfilling Goals

1. Darwin Payne, *Big D: Triumphs and Troubles of an American Supercity in the 20th Century* (Dallas: Three Forks Press, 2000), 378–9.

2. Lillian Bradshaw interview, August 19, 1998, 12–13.

3. *Dallas Time Herald*, April 28, 1967.

4. Wheeler and Jacobs, *Survey of the Public Library*, 18–19.

5. *The Dallas Morning News*, June 25, July 10, and August 9, 1967.

6. Ibid., January 5, 1968.

7. Ibid., October 1, 1968.

8. *Dallas Times Herald*, May 27, 1969; *White Rocker*, April 9, 1970.

9. *Dallas Times Herald*, January 15, January 22, and January 23, 1974; February 13, 1974; April 9, 1974.

10. Ibid., November 21, 1969; *The Dallas Morning News*, November 26, 1969.

11. *Oak Cliff Tribune*, December 24, 1969.

12. *Dallas Times Herald*, February 14, 1970.

13. *The Dallas Morning News*, December 25, 1968.
14. Interview with Linda Allmand, January 7, 2001.
15. *The Dallas Morning News*, August 8, 1969.
16. Ibid., October 14 and 17, 1971.
17. Ibid., June 18 and 28, 1972.
18. *Dallas Times Herald*, November 10, 1972.
19. *The Dallas Morning News*, January 9, 1973.
20. Minutes, Board of Trustees, September 10 and October 9, 1968.
21. *The Dallas Morning News*, July 26, 1972; *Dallas Times Herald*, August 1, 1972.
22. *The Dallas Morning News*, November 16, 1975.
23. *Dallas Times Herald*, June 27, 1973.
24. Introduction to Building Program, December 1973, quoted in Larry Grove: *Dallas Public Library: The First 75 Years* (Dallas: Dallas Public Library, 1977), 111.
25. *Oak Cliff Tribune*, June 12, 1974; *Dallas Times Herald*, August 24, 1975.
26. *Dallas Times Herald*, June 27, 1974; *The Dallas Morning News*, January 11, 1976.
27. Interview with Andrea Harris and Jan Moltzan, December 14, 2000.
28. *Dallas Times Herald*, December 31, 1975.
29. Ibid., April 1, 1976.
30. Interview with Jan Moltzan, December 14, 2000.
31. *Dallas Times Herald*, November 7, 1976; Grove, *Dallas Public Library*, 116–19.
32. Grove, *Dallas Public Library*, 89–107.

Chapter Eleven: Riding the Wave of Success

1. *Dallas Times Herald*, November 9, 1976.
2. Ibid., August 3, 1977.
3. *The Dallas Morning News*, January 2, 1977.
4. Interview with Richard Waters, February 15, 2001.
5. *Dallas Times Herald*, April 25, 1977.
6. Interview with Lillian Bradshaw, January 17, 2001.
7. Lillian Bradshaw, oral interview, August 19, 1998, 29–30.
8. *The Dallas Morning News*, December 22, 1977.
9. *Dallas Times Herald*, May 3, 1978, and June 4, 1978; *The Dallas Morning News*, May 11, 1978, and June 11, 1978.
10. *The Dallas Morning News*, July 12, 1981.
11. Ibid., April 18, 1982.
12. Ibid.; Bradshaw interview, August 19, 1998, 70–1.
13. Information provided by June Leftwich, January 2001.
14. Interview with Richard Waters, February 15, 2001.
15. Bradshaw interview, August 19, 1998, 37.
16. *The Dallas Morning News*, August 28, 1986.
17. Ibid., April 22, 1983.

18. Ibid., January 31, 1984.
19. Ibid., March 9, 1975.
20. Ibid., March 12, 2000.
21. Ibid.
22. Ibid., October 14, 1984.
23. Ibid., June 23, 1984.
24. *Dallas*, May 1985, 76.
25. *The Dallas Morning News*, November 24, 1985.
26. Ibid., April 27, 1985.
27. Ibid., April 7, 1986.
28. Ibid., January 25, 1986.
29. Interview with Andrea Harris and Jan Moltzan, December 14, 2000.

Chapter Twelve: A Library Under Siege

1. *The Dallas Morning News*, May 28, 1986.
2. Ibid., July 16, 1986.
3. Ibid., August 4, 1986.
4. Ibid., September 28, 1986.
5. Ibid., March 7, 1987.
6. Ibid., April 27, 1987.
7. Ibid., February 13, 1987.
8. Interview with Andrea Harris and Jan Moltzan, December 14, 2000.
9. Interview with Frances Bell, January 7, 2001.
10. *The Dallas Morning News*, June 8, 1987.
11. Ibid., May 3, 1988.
12. Ibid., September 23, 1987.
13. Ibid., April 13, 1988.
14. Ibid., April 14, 1988.
15. Ibid., October 3, 1988.
16. Ibid., October 18, 1988.
17. In addition to funds raised by the Friends, major gifts included $100,000 from Carl and Laura Brannin, $75,000 from the King Foundation, and $100,000 from an anonymous donor. Philanthropist Ida Green bequeathed $500,000 for programming. Ibid., May 18, 1989.
18. Ibid., January 3 and May 18, 1989.
19. Ibid., May 17 and 18, 1989.
20. Ibid., June 29, 1989.
21. Ibid., September 13, 1989.
22. Ibid., January 3, 1990.
23. Ibid., August 4, 1990.
24. Ibid., August 11, 1991.
25. Ibid., August 20, 1991.

26. Ibid., August 15, 1991.
27. Ibid., October 2, 1991.
28. Ibid., October 21, 1991.
29. Ibid., November 3, 1991.
30. Ibid., February 22, 1992.
31. Ibid., July 17, 1992.
32. Ibid., July 21, 1992.

Chapter Thirteen: Recovery

1. *The Dallas Morning News*, May 31, 1992.
2. Letter from David Morgan to Library Staff, August 31, 1993.
3. *The Dallas Morning News*, July 20, 1993.
4. Ibid., August 2, 1993.
5. Ibid.
6. Ibid., July 16, 1995.
7. Ibid., August 8, 1994.
8. Ibid., June 18, 1995.
9. Ibid., June 19, 1995.
10. Ibid., March 4 and April 19, 1995.
11. Ibid., April 19, 1995.
12. Ibid., November 1, 1996.
13. Ibid., November 2, 1996.
14. Ibid., January 9, 1996.
15. Ibid., August 30, 1996.
16. Ibid., March 26, 1997.
17. Ibid., November 2, 1996.
18. Ibid., March 9 and March 23, 1996.
19. Ibid., November 23, 1997.
20. Ibid., February 8, 1998.
21. Ibid., February 24, 1998.
22. Ibid.
23. Ibid., February 27, 1998.
24. Ibid., November 28, 1998.
25. Library Master Plan, II. Executive Summary, 2.
26. *The Dallas Morning News*, November 8, 1999.
27. Library Master Plan, II. Executive Summary, 20–1, 26–7.
28. Ibid., 9.
29. *The Dallas Morning News*, December 5, 1999.
30. Articles of Incorporation were adopted by the membership of the Friends in 1985.
31. Carol Roark, Foreword to exhibition catalogues.

32. For a full overview of the history of the Friends, see Lillian Moore Bradshaw, *Celebrating the First 50 Years: Friends of the Dallas Public Library 1950–2000* (Dallas: Dallas Public Library, 2000).

Chapter Fourteen: The Dallas Library Today . . . and Tomorrow

1. The library's operating budget increased from $16.9 million in FY95–96 to $22.8 million in FY00–01. Information provided by Ramiro S. Salazar.

2. These statistics, and more, can be found on the Dallas Public Library's excellent web page: www.dallaslibrary.org.

3. The Dallas Public Library received the Urban Libraries Council Highsmith Award of Excellence in 1999 for development and implementation of the Teen Center Program at the Highland Hills and Lakewood Branch libraries.

4. This sampling of programs is taken from the January 2001 issue of *Almanac*, the Dallas Public Library's monthly schedule of events.

5. Interview with Joe Bearden, January 11, 2001.

6. Interview with Ramiro S. Salazar, December 7, 2000.

7. Ibid.

8. Branch library service hours were expanded by four additional hours a week in January 1998. In response to a branch hours survey to gauge customer preferences, new branch hours were introduced in October 1999. Evening hours were extended at all branch libraries. Information provided by Ramiro S. Salazar.

9. Salazar interview.

10. Dallas Public Library received a $251,000 grant in 1999 from the Telecommunications Infrastructure Fund Board to improve Internet connectivity at all library locations. In 2000 it received a $103,550 grant from the Gates Library Foundation to enhance Internet connectivity at nine branch libraries; funding will also provide new computers and printers.

11. Bearden interview.

12. Salazar interview.

13. Bearden interview.

14. Interview with Lillian Bradshaw, January 17, 2001.

Index

Numbers in italics indicate illustrations.

E

F

T

U

V

W

Y